THE Jeanette MacDonald STORY

THE
Jeanette
MacDonald
STORY

James Robert Parish

MASON /CHARTER

NEW YORK 1976

Library of Congress Cataloging in Publication Data

Parish, James Robert.
  The Jeanette MacDonald story.

  1. MacDonald, Jeanette, 1907–1965. I. Title.
ML420.M135P4   791.43'02'80924   [B]   76–16553
ISBN 0–88405–360–1

For DOMINICK ABEL

ACKNOWLEDGMENTS

Research Associate, William R. Meyer.

With kind thanks to the indulgence of Earl Anderson, Dorothy Bachman, Constance Hope Berliner, DeWitt Bodeen, British Film Institute, Mrs. Loraine Burdick, Kingsley Canham, Joanna Christensen, John Robert Cocchi, Bosley Crowther, Louis and Rose Devon, Elinor Donahue, Morris Everett, Jr., Film Favorites (Charles Smith), David Finkle, Nat W. Finston, Chet Forrest, Senator Barry Goldwater, John Green, Stanley Green, Ken Harris, Claude Jarman, Jr., David Johnson, Allan Jones, Ken D. Jones, Eleanor Knowles, Miles Kreuger, Lotte Lehmann, William T. Leonard, Library of Lincoln Center: The Theatre Collection (Paul Myers, Curator), Library of the Academy of Motion Picture Arts & Sciences, Anita Loos, Doug McClelland, Patrick McGilligan, David McGillivray, Albert B. Manski, Alvin H. Marill, Samuel Marx, Mrs. Earl Meisinger, Peter Miglierini, Movie Poster Service (Bob Smith), Lloyd Nolan, Ken Norton, Horace W. Oster, *Philadelphia Evening Bulletin, Philadelphia Inquirer,* Michael R. Pitts, Peter Sanderson, Dr. Herman Schornstein, Mrs. Peter Smith, Florence Solomon, Charles K. Stumpf, T. Allan Taylor, Don Wigal, and Bob Wright.

With special appreciation to Richard Fernandez, Robert Friess, Clara Rhoades (President of the Jeanette MacDonald International Fan Club) and Tessa Williams.

Gene Raymond politely begged to be excused from participation in this project, which he felt would cause him too much personal sadness.

vii

PROLOGUE

"Get those bitches out of there!" snarled Louis B. Mayer at demure Jeanette MacDonald. It was a sunny day in the mid-1930s and the setting was the M-G-M lot. The persons in question were Joan Crawford and Norma Shearer, two other queens of the studio. They had snuck into the powder room, hoping to avoid continuing a tedious tour of the facilities with V.I.P. guests from Europe. A nonplussed Jeanette politely complied with her boss's rude order.

On another occasion, the most refined lady on the Metro payroll was treated to another major public indignity. As George Burns remembers it, "Gracie [Allen] and I and Jack [Benny] were invited by Louis B. Mayer to his house for a musicale to introduce M-G-M's new singing star, Jeanette MacDonald. At the house, Benny sat in front of me and I leaned over and said, 'Now Jack, when she starts singing, I don't want you to laugh!' When Jeanette started to sing, he broke up laughing. So I wasn't the only one who could make Jack Benny laugh. Jeanette MacDonald could, too."

Humiliating episodes such as these were indeed responsible for Jeanette's candid self-evaluation, "I did not have a particularly easy time achieving anything in my career." And it was true. Her life was a battle against odds, tempered by an optimistic nature and a strong faith in God. On one occasion she confessed, "I do believe to a degree in our destiny . . . it helps to mold."

Yet her most rewarding victory was not the cultivation of her international fame and adoration, or the accumulation of sizable wealth. Instead, it was the joy of her wedded life to actor-singer-songwriter Gene Raymond. As Miss MacDonald pointed out, "I had the greatest achievement in marriage . . . one reaches for the highest star." Her nearly thirty-year love affair with Mr. Raymond was as incredibly real and beautiful as her almost always benevolent nature (no matter what the vast array of disbelievers insisted).

Perhaps the finest tribute to Jeanette MacDonald was told to me by concert agent Constance Hope Berliner, who knew and loved the star. Recently she theorized on why the "MacRaymonds" had such a happy and long marriage: "I emulated her in trying not to build myself up to my husband, but to build him up to everybody else. . . . [Jeanette's] linen in her bathroom was always monogrammed—not 'J Mac R,' it was 'J.A.R.' She was 'Jeanette Anna Raymond' in her home. And when the car was called, it was Mr. Raymond's car. She had a necklace that had written on it 'Jeanette Raymond.' " When Mrs. Berliner would query Jeanette about all those little things that spelled love, the famed singer would reply, "Well, you know, he's such a wonderful boy. And that's the least I can do. I'm one of the lucky women who got a legitimate, decent man."

It is said there are two kinds of people in the world: the givers and the takers. This biography is about Jeanette MacDonald, the Giver.

THE
Jeanette
MacDonald
STORY

CHAPTER ONE

At the turn of the century, when the typical American metropolis was suffering from widespread corruption, there were persistent cries for social and political reform. For example, in New York in November, 1894, Tammany Hall politicians who had been a major corrupting influence in Manhattan for decades were finally voted out of power. Major cities were focal points for demonstrations favoring pure food and drug legislation, child labor laws, workmen's compensation, women's rights and numerous other life-improving causes. Writers like Upton Sinclair and Frank Norris were turning out novels that tiraded against the many evils perpetrated by oil companies, mining organizations, Chicago stockyards and meat-packing plants, the frauds in journalism and education and, in particular, against the life-crushing factory production lines which sprang from the Industrial Revolution of the late 1800s.

To many sociologists, journalists and novelists, and to other interested observers of the early twentieth century, the city was so big, was expanding so.fast and was so full of corruption, exploitation and everyday inequity that a revolution of some sort seemed sure to occur. While groups such as the Industrial Workers of the World tried to organize labor, journalists like John Reed publicized the Paterson Silk Strike, publishers like Max Eastman produced radical magazines, and Socialist Eugene V. Debs campaigned for President of the United States, the chaos of the expected revolution never came in America.

A city such as Philadelphia was never disturbed by the riots that

1

occurred in the decade before World War I. If the historic situs was not exactly a city of brotherly love, it was certainly an area where a sort of familial equilibrium ruled the populace. Granted Philadelphia was not entirely free of unrest. There were labor strikes by both skilled and unskilled workers, often spearheaded by the Industrial Workers of the World, agitation by and against radicals and foreigners, and patriotic rhetoric that divided rather than unified.

The Philadelphia of 1905 was not severely different from the Philadelphia that settled down in the 1850s. In these years, Philadelphia's economic classes occupied basically an almost standard territory. Likewise, the division between urban areas and suburbs was spared radical alteration. By 1900, industry had long settled in its place, and the boiling points reached more than a half century earlier had long since fizzled into acceptance.

Then too, the nation's reform movements may not have shaken the foundations of Philadelphia, but they nevertheless made peaceful inroads into the system. City planning in Philadelphia constructively began in 1905 when the august City Council accepted a citizens' committee proposal to build the Fairmount Parkway boulevard connecting City Hall with a proposed art museum at the edge of the park. Many cities like Philadelphia were adopting the same notions of city beautification.

Philadelphia Mayor John E. Rayburn soon requested that the Board of Survey conduct studies on how to unsnarl the typically urban downtown traffic situation, and formed a group of businessmen to devise plans for the city. It was not until 1919 that a regular planning commission was charted in Philadelphia, but the city was on progressive wheels. It was moving toward a better life for all, even if there were occasional setbacks, compounded by persistent municipal graft and indecisiveness.

As today, the influx of immigrants into America in the late 1800s and the early 1900s caused much social friction. As these new citizens searched for the alleged gold-paved streets described by oracles and fleshed out by their own dreams, there was tremendous resentment from natural-born Americans and the immigrants who had come earlier than the latest batch of wandering human beings. Downtown Philadelphia businessmen, and the Chamber of Commerce in particular, were fearful of the alien influence on their ever-expanding city, once the seat

2

of the nation's government. To combat what they considered a serious threat, they organized programs of Americanization for the foreigners, hoping to bring some of them into the mainstream of typical American culture. Although the ever-present political bosses of the city required that all municipal programs include specific benefits for their communities, they were not against educational expansion. The dream appeared on the idealized horizon that the standard of living could be brought to a humane plateau through education.

After several years of seesawing progress, the programs were put into practice. Night classes were offered to drop-outs and to immigrants, the sick and handicapped profited from special aid, and it was proposed that children be treated as individual entities, and not regarded as part and parcel of a mass of faces known as a class.

Philadelphia's Superintendent of Schools, Edwin C. Broome (1874–1950), in the post-World War I period was determined to extend the reaches of public education and to fulfill the needs of each student. Unfortunately, although Philadelphia's schools did become more flexible in an attempt to accommodate a wider range of students, they could do nothing really to break down the ghettoization prominent in the burgeoning metropolis. The rich lived with the rich in the lush Rittenhouse Park area downtown or in the still "uncontaminated" suburban areas, the poor with the poor, ad infinitum. The public school offered the student assorted alternatives: a college course, a general curriculum, or commercial and industrial plans. But this was not enough to dissuade the affluent upper classes from a very Eastern United States tradition of private schooling. By the 1920s there were all sorts of alternative private institutions populated with the children of the wealthy. The fears of early nineteenth-century Philadelphia reformers would be realized all too dramatically in the twentieth century by this gross segregation of the Philadelphia social classes and racial-ethnic centers.

By the 1900s, neighborhoods were composed of similar economic and national origin types. People tended to mix with what can roughly be described as "their own kind." With hope of economic improvement, educational and urban planning, the segregation, in a way, provided a sense of belonging to newly Americanized families; it gave a communal feeling as well to Philadelphians who could lean against a neighbor's fence and lend a sympathetic ear to understood

3

and experienced problems of a social and ethnic twin.

Distinctive neighborhoods cropped up in Philadelphia. Districts were known for one ethnic group or another, or could be labeled "suburbs," or housed the city's business and industry, thus becoming cut off from residential areas. This was the spiraling phenomenon of the twentieth-century city, and by the early 1900s, Philadelphia was a modern metropolis. Tracts of industry or ethnic areas appeared this way in turn-of-the-century Philadelphia: the downtown section ran from Vine Street to South Street, northern industrial suburbs east of Sixth Street became a mill town, the South Philadelphia Peninsula was an entry port for foreigners, to the west of the Schuylkill River grew bedroom suburbs, and also to the northwest, extending past old mills and rotting pre-Civil War housing.

It was in a middle-class neighborhood of West Philadelphia at 5123 Arch Street that Jeanette Anna MacDonald was born on Thursday, June 18, 1903.* Her parents, Daniel and Anna M. (Wright) MacDonald, were twice parents before Jeanette's birth: There was Elsie born about 1896, and Edith Blossom in 1899. Although Elsie and Edith Blossom (called Blossom) were born at 3313 Wallace Street ("near the railroad tracks" Blossom would later recall) in the vicinity of 33rd and Spring Garden streets in Philadelphia, the family had moved by the time Jeanette was born. The MacDonalds were then situated in a comfortable three-story red brick house that was built by Daniel MacDonald, a building contractor responsible for the creation of the entire neighborhood. Some sources insist Mr. MacDonald was not quite up to planning housing developments, but simply managed a woodworking construction company, and further assert that the Mac-Donald ménage occupied only a two-story house on Arch Street.

Years later, after Jeanette was internationally famous as the better half of M-G-M's immensely popular Jeanette MacDonald-Nelson

---

*As with many celebrities, birth years were a matter of convenience. Jeanette always insisted 1907 was her year of birth. The inscription on her crypt gives 1907 as her birth year.

4

Eddy singing duo, she recalled her Arch Street home to a reporter. Upon stepping inside the house, one entered a reception hall, papered in a dark and (to Jeanette) uninteresting red. To the left was a square, uncomfortable and ugly settee. Hung over it was a mahogany-rimmed mirror with hooks holding coats and seldom-used articles of clothing. In one corner there was a large chair with an adjustable back, and next to it a replica of a turtle. The parlor contained an upright piano and a bay window. A sign hung on the wall which read, "May the Lord Bless This Christian Hearth."

Although the MacDonalds lived in a normal middle-class neighborhood, Daniel MacDonald was one of the few home dwellers actually to own his house. Presumably his affiliation with district planners gave him something of an edge over his less fortunate neighbors. The MacDonald home, as pictured earlier, was sparsely furnished, and seems to have embodied the traditional American puritan spirit which pervaded so many turn-of-the-century North American households. Mr. and Mrs. MacDonald were devout Presbyterians (the entire family attended the Tennent Presbyterian Church on the corner of 51st and Arch streets), and they raised their children with an impartiality that some feel may have slightly hurt Jeanette. Being the third of the MacDonalds' children, the youngest, she was in need of the babying given the youngest offspring of typical parents. Perhaps she never got that special protection and was, in fact, left alone to the point where she had to develop extreme initiative to obtain what she wanted, or even to be noticed.

"Jessie," as Jeanette was frequently called by her family (in memory of grandmother Jessie), discovered early the necessary steps to the spotlight. One day Blossom—her favorite sister—taught Jeanette a song, the "Glory Hymn," and little Jessie would go around singing the newly learned tune in public and private, thus commanding the attention she desired. According to Jeanette, "My first memories are of dancing up and down in front of the family phonograph, singing arias with accompaniment of various prima donnas' records and imagining I was really standing behind the grand opera or concert footlights." It was not too long before her fond dream came true.

But the thing she most remembered about her early life in Philadelphia was, of all things, ice cream. "We used to go to a corner store to get it in a dish. We had two poodles at home—I had to wash them every Saturday, incidentally—and if anybody said 'Where's the dish?' they would come racing down from upstairs, or wherever they were. They knew it meant ice cream." Every Sunday, rain or shine, Jeanette walked to the drug store near the Nixon Theatre on 52nd Street after Sunday school for ice cream.

Although the MacDonald family was not descended from anything resembling a show-business background on either side, every week the family would walk to the nearby Nixon Theatre to enjoy the stage shows. Jeanette had the most fun, and later remembered, "Rose and Ramella Ponselle were there one week and my parents took me to hear them and oh, they had such glorious voices! It was a wonderful experience." Being of stern Scottish stock, it is a bit surprising that ultra-conservative Daniel MacDonald made a habit of taking his wife and children to any type of theater. More surprising, at first, is the fact that Daniel never seemed to strenuously object to his children's interest in show business. All three girls, Elsie, Blossom and tiny Jeanette, were, in Anna MacDonald's words, "musically inclined." But even then, Jessie was something special. In motherly but rather revealing terms, Mrs. MacDonald once said:

> My two oldest daughters, Elsie and Blossom, were no longer babies and I was just breathing a sigh of relief over my lessened responsibilities as a mother when I discovered that my family was not yet completed. But I simply applied the old adage "Everything happens for the best," and began making plans for the new baby.
>
> Jeanette was a darling baby—big-eyed and of sunny disposition. . . . Oh, she wasn't too good to be true—she managed to get into enough mischief so that we were well aware of her existence.
>
> When most babies her age were crying she was singing. She had a toy piano and she would sit on the porch and play it and sing by the hour to her grandfather—and to the neighbors.

Elsie and Blossom were, even at a tender age, interested in their baby sister's musical development. Elsie was something of a child prodigy, as she played piano by ear, and Blossom always remembered song lyrics; together they taught Jessie the songs she would sing on the stairs, on the porch, in the sandbox in the park. A park caretaker told Mrs. MacDonald one afternoon, "I've been here a long time and I've seen plenty of them sing but I never saw such a little one sing and never heard anyone sing so loud." The little one was about two at the time, and by the time she was four, Jeanette had enrolled in sister Blossom's dancing class.

The story behind Jeanette's first appearance at dance class follows a logical progression from spotlight to spotlight. One day this youngest of three children decided she did not want to live with her family anymore, so she ran away. The journey did not last long—she was brought back home by Casey, the butter-and-egg man. By this time a frantic Daniel and Anna had called both the police and fire departments in an effort to locate their prodigal daughter. Probably feeling that a dance class might stem Jessie's desire to travel, Mrs. MacDonald permitted Blossom to take the runaway to class to keep her mind occupied. Blossom dressed her little sister in a treasured sailor suit with a big bow, and while walking to class, taught her sister the words to "Old Mother Hubbard."

It just so happened that Blossom's class was presenting a show with Old Mother Hubbard as one of the characters. Singing loud and proud, with song emanating from her little heart, Jeanette was invited to play Mother Hubbard in the pageant. It was more exciting to the child than the time she had made her impromptu debut at church when she broke into a popular tune. (Of that occasion Blossom would recall, "Can you imagine a small little redhead, so disappointed in the lack of applause following her first solo in church that she began clapping her own small hands?")

There was joy on Arch Street that day. Tiny Jeanette was excited about playing at the Academy of Music in the show. There was only one minor problem. On their way home from rehearsal, full of the exuberance indigenous to budding show-business careers, Jeanette lost her gold bracelet. Mrs. MacDonald scolded Blossom for allowing her sister to be so careless. Wanting to atone, enterprising Blossom went to a neighborhood theater that evening and performed a song and dance, winning a $2.50 prize. She ran home and presented the money to her surprised mother. Everything was fixed and Mrs. MacDonald resigned herself to being, not a stage mother, but the mother of two girls who wanted to be on the stage.

In 1907 Jessie MacDonald made her debut as a rather pixieish Old Mother Hubbard. By then she had matured from a slightly chubby little baby into everybody's image of daddy's pretty young girl. She may have been the center of attention even then, but she never forgot that it was her doting sisters who provided her with the needed push into the spotlight:

> I sort of thrived on the accomplishments of Elsie and Blossom. The whole family was so proud of them. I thought they were the most wonderful girls in the world. I was just young enough to be a hero worshipper. And they were proud of me. I remember once I went to dancing school with mother to call for Blossom. Blossom insisted I sing for her teacher—she wanted to "show off" her baby sister. I sang and the teacher invited me to sing at the annual school recital.

There may be a variety of versions of just how Jeanette got to the music-and-dance school, yet the story always concludes the same, and the evidence that the family supported their youngest member's dream of a life of singing and dancing is consistent. The four-year-old redhead was on her way.

By the time she was six, Jeanette was showing off her soprano voice in "kid" charity operas staged by James H. Littlefield and his wife, Caroline. Other children in the operas were the Littlefields' daughter Catherine, later a well-known danseuse, and Ann Pennington, who became famous on Broadway for her dimpled knees. Naturally Jeanette was the "leading woman," and sisters Blossom and Elsie did "bits" in the shows.

Mrs. Minnie Barry, who sewed costumes for the mini operas, recalled how an enthusiastic Jeanette "brought down the house" with a real Scotch song and nearly deserted it with her "bear song."

> Jeanette used to huddle in the corners at rehearsals during the bear number. She knew the bear was only Mr. Littlefield in a bearskin, but as soon as he would put on the

8

bear head little Jeanette's imagination ran away with her. She never could seem to get herself to trust the animal. Thought maybe it might be a really-truly bear after all.

Catherine Littlefield, who was not quite three years old then, danced while Jeanette sang to the bear, and both children had promised before they stepped out on the stage that they wouldn't be afraid.

But that was a promise neither "trouper" could keep! The "bear" growled, Catherine jumped across the footlights and Jeanette sprinted right off the stage in the middle of her specialty number.

Even though Miss MacDonald and her sisters were seasoned stage performers before reaching their teens, they were not permitted to rest on their laurels. Since the family did not have a maid, the MacDonald children had to share the housework, scrubbing stairs, dusting, making beds and washing floors, all for a weekly allowance of ten cents. If the wages of a houseworker did not convince the energetic trio that show business was a more rewarding career, nothing would. But it was the master stroke of Daniel and Anna MacDonald not to allow the children's success to swell their egos. In the ensuing years, their stage wages would bolster the family coffers, but Mr. MacDonald never let the girls forget who they were.

Little Jeanette was not above continuing her neighborhood "appearances" once she began singing and dancing for pay. She used to entertain one of the neighbors, a crippled old man named Mr. Maetrich. She would visit him at his house and sing her own special versions of operas she had just learned. The grateful gentleman was charmed by his songbird neighbor, and told her that one day she would be a famous opera star. Jeanette could "sing" in French and Italian, garbled sounds which seemed foreign to her and most closely resembled those sung by Caruso and others on the records to which she constantly listened.

The MacDonald girls also offered little presentations in the family's cellar, to add a breath of fresh air to the summer heat. They used empty coal bins for dressing rooms. And yet Mrs. MacDonald could never comprehend how their starched white dresses would become so dirty. After all, they were not mining coal, only dressing in coal bins.

During one performance Blossom and Jeanette had a disagreement over something—perhaps one was upstaging the other. The usually amiable siblings then started a fight that would have surprised even those who knew the girls best. Hearing a ruckus, Mrs. MacDonald scurried down to the basement to investigate. She found the older and bigger Blossom sitting on her little sister, choking the life out of her. As the smaller girl's face was turning blue, Blossom realized just what she was doing. She immediately stopped and held little Jeanette in her arms, sobbing hysterically. This is how close the sisters were.

On weekend nights during the school year, Jeanette and Blossom played Philadelphia's vaudeville houses, earning about ten dollars an evening for their singing act.

Although Mr. MacDonald was liberal about allowing his children to perform in arenas still considered immoral by many, there was a hard and steadfast rule that on Sunday, the MacDonalds were a strictly traditional middle-class family. That meant no performing, no rehearsing, no shop talk. The additional income was certainly welcome, but the girls' religious training was not to be neglected. The father's influence on this issue was to remain an important spiritual factor in Jeanette's life. A belief in God, nurtured by Daniel MacDonald and the Presbyterian Church, gave the aspiring performer the necessary belief in herself to keep striving for the heights of success she eventually achieved. In later life she did not forget her spiritual training, and taught Sunday School at the First Presbyterian Church in Los Angeles.

Jeanette's academic education was not shirked either. "Jimmie" —as Jeanette was often called by her classmates—attended the Dunlap Grammar School in Philadelphia, where she gained yet another nickname, "Broomstick Legs." For the most part, she enjoyed grammar-school life, and achieved good grades in many subjects. After school, she would frequently stop in at the neighborhood drugstore for her beloved ice cream. In the rear center of the store was a huge mirror which served as the backing for the prescription counter behind it. William B. Riegel, who then owned the shop, would later recall to Louis Devon, who purchased the store in 1928 (at the same time he was writing film reviews for *The Philadelphia Ledger*), "Oh yes, Jeanette would come in nearly every day and I would catch her posing and pirouetting before the mirror, tossing her blonde hair and having a great time. 'What are you trying to do?' I would say. 'Practicing. I'm going to be a dancer.' 'A dancer! You'll never be a dancer with those skinny legs.' 'I will so. And I'll be a star.' "

It was in grammar school that Jeanette fell in love for the first time. The man in question was a carrot-topped youth named Raymond Scott. One day Jeanette was so excited about her love for Raymond that she decided to spill everything in a passionate love note. But she did not trust her own ability to convey heartfelt feelings in the proper way. So she copied a letter out of the newspaper. Unfortunately, the letter reproduced in the paper was evidence in a breach of promise suit, so one may assume the spice of the impassioned communication far outweighed the sugar.

Jeanette threw the note toward her "lover," but she did not know her own strength, and the "red hot" piece of paper sailed straight into the hands of the teacher, Miss Palmer. When the note was read, the teacher turned red with anger, and its author was sent home as punishment. But it was not the last of the *affaire de coeur* with Raymond.

By the time she was nine, Jeanette's romance with Raymond Scott was the gossip of the neighborhood. Many people commented on how much they resembled one another, with their dutch-bobbed red hair, and how nice they looked together as a couple, gliding across the floor in dancing school.

Since Jeanette was such a pretty young thing, it was natural that she should have other suitors. One such interloper was Jack Graugh. Raymond and Jack were pals. It was not the first time a friendship was smashed by a woman. One afternoon the two buddies were taking target practice with a .22 in the basement of Jack's house. Not understanding the competition that was gnawing at their bond of companionship, Raymond put himself right in the firing line by rushing over to straighten the target before the shooting began. Jack took advantage of the target he wanted to hit more than the one with the circles, and pumped a bullet into Raymond's leg. It was several days before the physicians realized the wound was not as serious as originally believed. Despite this good news, Jeanette still envisioned herself as the classical fair maiden being fought over by two handsome, courageous young men. She vowed to be good and not stick her tongue out at anybody, to pay penance for Raymond's "bullet through the heart." She would become a nun.

11

One evening Jeanette's plans to become a servant of God were excitingly shattered. A vaudeville performer named Al White called on the MacDonalds, and to the surprise of all, offered the role of prima donna in the child act he was then forming to the youngest MacDonald sister. White wanted to take Jeanette with him for a summer engagement touring Eastern resort towns. It was like a dream come true. School would be out by then. She could become a real pro.

White's act consisted of six children, two girls and four boys, and was called "Six Sunny Song Birds." It was agreed that Mrs. MacDonald would travel with the troupe. No one was more pleased about Jeanette's success than Blossom, who had aspirations to a show-business career herself. White's "kiddie revue" toured Ocean Wood and Atlantic City in New Jersey and Hershey and Harrisburg in Pennsylvania. By the end of the summer, if legend can be believed, Jeanette was the star of the show.

Despite the summer adulation, by the fall Jeanette was back in the classroom with her peers, much to the regret of Al White, who considered her a performing natural. It was at this point that she ran afoul of a prune-faced teacher. This straightlaced instructor was so highly offended that such a little girl would be subjected to the crass, immoral world of show business that she took her complaint directly to the Board of Education. Again it must be stated that the MacDonalds were an unusual family for encouraging their daughters to perform in public. At the time, vaudeville was considered an improper atmosphere for adults, and allowing a child to not only attend shows but perform herself must certainly have raised more than one set of austere eyebrows in Philadelphia. Perhaps only second to Boston in a reputation for conservatism, Philadelphians were liberal enough to permit Daniel MacDonald to run for political office, and enjoy life as a respected citizen.

Years later Jeanette remembered the incident, still hurt by the excruciating experience.

As long as I live, I shall never forget the indignity of standing there before those people and answering the insinuating questions they put to me. I could hardly speak, I was trembling with such rage when they asked if Father beat me, if Mother beat me and if they took the money I earned away from me by force. I couldn't understand what it was all about. We had had such fun with the act, Mother and I!

And now we were almost like criminals. Answering those impudent questions put by total strangers while that woman sat on the sidelines and smirked. How I hated her! Yet I felt she hated me equally as much. Who painted my face? When did I go to bed? Did I ever see grown people smoking and drinking? Had I heard any "bad language"?

Of course, I tried not to show the outrage I felt. And I suppose I answered the questions satisfactorily. At least, the report that came back stated that the body found me a very nice little girl and that my education had not suffered and that I had been exposed to no unmoral influences.

Even after that nerve-racking ordeal, Jeanette's trial was not over. Although she had convinced the Board of Education that there was nothing wrong in her performing on the stage, she had yet to be rid of her accuser. Defeated by the Board, the woman decided to wage a personal war against an eleven-year-old girl. The reasons for such highly neurotic actions can only be surmised. Was the woman frustrated with her own life? Had she been forbidden to go on the stage as a youngster, and like so many adults, determined to carry on the sins of her parents? Did she have a vaudevillian lover who had jilted her for a chorus girl? Or was the story of Jeanette's tribulation made exceedingly melodramatic by a dusty memory and the wishes of a well-meaning publicist? Was the woman in question really concerned about the little girl's well-being?

It is reported that the feline ogre continually made a nuisance of herself, showing up in the front row of all of Jeanette's performances. She would stare intently at the girl, and eventually made the young performer nervous. This is thought to be a root of the stage fright Jeanette suffered in later years.

This woman's vendetta caused Jeanette to lose a potentially profitable job in New York City. Child acts were quite the rage at the time, with Gus Edwards' group and another called the Rosebuds being very successful. Al White had ambitions for his "Six Sunny Song Birds." He was fortunate enough to land several lucrative contracts in New York. Naturally he wanted his little star to play the engagements. Jeanette

13

and her mother journeyed to Manhattan only to receive word from the Gerry Society that an unsigned telegram had indicated Miss Mac-Donald was only eleven, four years short of the legal performing age. The MacDonalds did not have to speculate long on the authoress of the telegram, but there was nothing to be done. Jeanette was indeed only eleven, so it was back to Philadelphia, to await another shot at the big time.

Perhaps if a student is really fortunate he has a Mr. Chips or a Miss Dove guiding some of his formal education. Jeanette's teaching joy proved to be Miss Edna Clear, her seventh-grade teacher. Years later, in 1952, on TV's "This Is Your Life," Jeanette would reminisce about how she adored Miss Clear and that whenever she and her friends played teacher-students, Jeanette always insisted on being Miss Clear. The fact that Miss Clear enjoyed singing and sometimes performed for her students endeared her further to the idolizing Jeanette.

A little while after these incidents, while Jeanette-Jessie-Jimmie was pondering her career, or lack of it, at home, someone who would play a major role in Jeanette MacDonald's life only less important than her husband, Gene Raymond, moved to Philadelphia. A family had broken up in Rhode Island, and a divorced mother moved to the city of brotherly love with her fourteen-year-old son to start life anew. The husband remained in Rhode Island, remarried, and later had a daughter. The young man did not complete high school; evidently he was not impressed by a liberal Philadelphia public school system that was already starting to show the strain of changing too much too fast with too little support. Perhaps the teen-ager did not care for teachers like the one who hounded Jeanette. He, too, had a certain fondness for singing.

Having also the burden of contributing his share of income to his mother, young Nelson Eddy quit school. He tried making use of Philadelphia's experimental night school, and also took correspondence courses. But mostly Nelson went from job to job, from clerk in a shipping room, later to obituary writer, then to ad salesman for *The Philadelphia Press,* police reporter for *The Public Ledger* and *Bulletin,* copywriter for N. W. Ayer & Sons, and so on.

It is fascinating to speculate on whether or not Jeanette and Nelson's paths intertwined at all during their Philadelphia days. Although they did not attend the same high school (Jeanette went to the

West Philadelphia School for Girls), perhaps they passed each other at a football game, or sat in the same auditorium for a vaudeville show or a concert. Maybe Nelson thought of taking lessons from Jeanette's voice teacher, Wassilli Leps, but decided it would be too much of a financial burden on the Eddy's modest existence. The possibilities of such encounters are nearly endless.

While Nelson was busy dropping out of high school, Jeanette (she was now too old to be called "Jim-Jam," based on her initials, J.A.M.) was caught up in a flurry of secondary school activity. Sister Blossom attended West Philadelphia Girls High for a spell but dropped out because she was "too busy with weekend jobs, singing and dancing." Aside from performing with Jeanette, Blossom also had an act with older sister Elsie, who would play the piano as the middle sister sang.

"I was getting along pretty well," Jeanette once recalled. "I was my class representative and I was getting involved in politics and I felt I was pretty important." Having lost the thorn in her side who persecuted her through grammar school, Jeanette could concentrate on her studies and extracurricular activities. Her best subjects at West Philadelphia High were history, English and French; yellowed report cards reveal columns with grades in the 80s and 90s in those subjects, even though Jeanette remembers herself a poor student. (Classmate Rose Landesberg, who later wed drugstore owner and film critic Louis Devon, recently remembered, "I'd say she was an average student, but always talked about the stage and dancing.")

Once Jeanette received a mark of fifty-two in algebra, hating the subject every step of the way. The teacher asked her why the grade was so low, and Jeanette countered by wondering why a knowledge of algebra was so necessary. The puzzled instructor had no answer, but asked her something to the effect of "Don't you want to pass anyway?"

Miss Virginia Henderson, a small, thin woman with fine features and white hair, wore beautiful jewelry, and had a wonderful sense of humor. She also was the very fine musical director at West Philadelphia High School. Years later she would speak of a prize pupil.

> I used to teach Jeanette. She was always a perfect little lady and sang beautifully. She was intelligent and a good pupil, too.
> She was a member of our Music Club and during her

15

sophomore year we selected her as the girl possessing the best voice of the year. That honor won her the main soprano role in our play that year, a part usually only given to girls in the senior class.

She was excellent in dramatics too, and her voice gave indications of future development.

Dark-haired Miss Stella Cullen, head of the gym department and an administrative assistant in the principal's office, also remembered the talented teen-age girl.

None of us had any idea it [her voice] would be developed to the extent it has been. Jeanette was exceedingly popular here. She was always so graceful and obliging.

It was rather unusual that such a beautiful girl should combine so many other qualities in her makeup. The fact that she was one of the directors of the Students' Association proved her popularity both with pupils and teachers.

Apparently the old cliché that an active, intelligent girl who possessed the leadership qualities of a Jeanette MacDonald got commended rather than kissed is applicable here. She once said she never had a date in high school, being too busy with academic and extracurricular activities and performing.

The teen-age experience often carries the label "the awkward years," and this phrase certainly describes Jeanette's teens. She was too tall (having reached her full height of 5 feet, 4 inches by the age of thirteen) and too skinny for her age. Where it was once possible to laugh at Elsie and Blossom's romantic entanglements through the distance of childhood, Jeanette was now jealous of the male attention her sisters received. At this time she was too young to socialize with her sisters and their friends.

By the time Jeanette almost had her first date, Elsie had eloped, and Blossom was carving out a career as a chorine in New York. The youngest sister considered herself a failure in comparison to them. But one fine day school chum Marie Prescott decided to hold a birthday gala. It was arranged that an enigma named Freddy would escort Jeanette to the occasion. On the evening of the big affair, she dressed

16

herself in her finest clothes, feeling unhappy that she had nothing "adult" to wear. She looked in the mirror at the gangly girl in the cotton bloomers, which buttoned to the gathered cambric upper, the legs in their pure white stockings, the feet encased in low-heeled patent leather pumps. After a while she picked a dress, put it on, and sat at the edge of the bed waiting for Freddy. At 10:30 Freddy was nowhere to be found so, tearfully, Jeanette undressed and hoped for better days.

The next day she confronted Freddy in the school courtyard. Brusquely he told her to "go to hell" and that was seemingly the end of the incident. But not quite. Years later, when Jeanette was establishing herself on Broadway, an older and presumably more sympathetic Freddy telephoned her and requested a date. "You remember me," he said. She admitted she did and then asked him what their parting words were those long years before. "I told you to go to hell, didn't I?" "Yes," sneered Jeanette, "and that's what I'm telling you." She slammed the phone down in his ear and closed the door to amorous Freddy forever.

There were other disappointments in Jeanette's high-school years. Rose Landesberg remembers she and Jeanette were among those rehearsing *The Mikado* under Miss Henderson's direction. Jeanette was to be Yum Yum, but the venture did not receive the necessary financial support from the School and Home Association and it was never staged.

While Jeanette was being rejected by Freddy and losing the plum operetta role, the world continued on its own course. Archduke Ferdinand of Austria was assassinated by revolutionaries in Serbia, which sparked World War I or, as it was known then, the "Great War" or the "World War." New American idols like Mary Pickford, Charlie Chaplin and Douglas Fairbanks were making public appearances at rallies in support of the war effort; once the United States entered the global battle, they sold war bonds and even made short propaganda films about the dreaded Hun. Meanwhile, anarchists were blowing up buildings and Eugene V. Debs was jailed for being a Socialist in war time. Yet Philadelphia remained essentially calm, standing a bit above it all.

This is not to suggest that there was no political activity or strife in the city of brotherly love. Building contractor Daniel MacDonald had been following the political scene for years. Deciding to be a doer rather than a talker, he sought political office. It is unclear exactly when

17

he made his initial thrust into politics, or to what office he aspired. But it is a fairly safe assumption that he was a staunch Republican, as his youngest daughter was to be throughout life. Jeanette's interest in politics dates back to her high-school years, and there is little doubt her father's influence swayed her maturing outlook to the right.

While dad was politicking and Elsie was playing at married life (she would go to the altar three times), Blossom was in New York as the prize pupil of Al White, employed as a show dancer. Jeanette was living the dual life of a high-school girl and practicing her singing and dancing. She devoted more time and energy to dancing than to singing. Consequently, her feet developed rhythm before her voice cultivated adult style. Ironically, Jeanette was not overly fond of dancing. In fact, she would later resent it when her reputation as a Broadway dancer in the Twenties prevented the securing of coveted singing roles. Yet she felt it a necessary skill for anyone with stage aspirations. She was a rather unique soft-shoe and tap dancer. Dancing with feet wide apart made her movements ingratiatingly odd. A year or so into the future, Jeanette, known as "the kid," would certainly be an odd duck in a chorus line. But it made her stand out and gravitated her toward stardom.

CHAPTER TWO

The story of Jeanette's journey to New York to audition for Ned Wayburn's *Demi Tasse Revue* is hazy. One source claims Blossom wrote home pleading for her younger sister to come to town and land one of the then bountiful dancing jobs. Jeanette left, won a job, and the rest is history. Not quite.

It is also possible that after Daniel MacDonald was defeated for political office the family had moved lock, stock and barrel to New York. (Oddly enough, once the MacDonalds got to New York, Jeanette did not live in the home of her parents. It is probable she first resided in a theatrical rooming house with Blossom, before taking her own apartment in the Bronx sometime in 1923.) One source said that Jeanette enrolled in Washington Irving High School on New York's 15th Street in November, 1919, and by February of the next year had transferred to Julia Richman High School in the upper Sixties.

Jeanette was not happy at leaving West Philadelphia High School, so one may assume with a small degree of certainty that she left for permanent residence in New York with no prospective jobs. Perhaps her father had secured employment, or thought his chances were better in a city where he was not a defeated political candidate.

At any rate, Jeanette MacDonald earned her first stage job in New York in late 1919. Blossom was already signed to perform in the show, and brought sis with her one rehearsal afternoon to audition for Wayburn. Blossom dressed the nervous girl in one of her own dresses and a sealskin coat. She put her own black straw hat with pink roses

(Jeanette's favorite color) on the auditionee's head and took her to the boss. Although Blossom's sealskin coat kept getting under her feet, causing her to waddle, Jeanette held on to her courage as she stood in Wayburn's office requesting a job.

Wayburn studied her and asked her what she could do. She said she could sing and dance. "Well, sing," he ordered. She did. Unfortunately she was out of key. One source says Wayburn halted her and told the "songstress" to go into her dance, convinced she would never be a singer. Others say Jeanette saw Wayburn was not impressed with her singing, and when she could not reach the high notes, began dancing and fell flat on her face. Still others persist that Wayburn asked her if she knew how to do a time step, and if so, to demonstrate. Jeanette, it seems, did not know what a time step was, but made do. (This seems unlikely, as she had been given dancing lessons by Blossom at a tender age, and had studied with Al White in Philadelphia for at least five or six years.)

Whatever the real truth is, Wayburn gave her a job in the chorus —way in the back. Part of her duties on stage was to sit in the middle of the floor dressed as an Indian and get hit in the head with a coffee can. It was a strange Broadway beginning for the future queen of screen operetta. But it is said Jeanette was not so much out of character in those days. She was, at first, an oddity to experienced showgirls, who referred to her as "the kid."

Her cotton stockings and lack of makeup gave Jeanette a rather eccentric, ingenuous appearance in a show world of glitter and gold. On rainy days people on the street could hear Jeanette coming in her knee-length galoshes, but they could not discern her very well, as a huge black cotton umbrella obscured the view of the fresh-faced young woman. Her rehearsal outfit consisted of bloomers that were puffed up like blimps, a middy blouse, and either Mrs. MacDonald or Blossom or both.

Jeanette had quite a time persuading her parents to let her do the show. Mrs. MacDonald marvelled at her daughter's power over wills. She had an answer for everything. Mrs. MacDonald later wrote:

> She knew she would meet opposition to her plans when she reached home so she figured out just what our objections would be and was ready with a refutation for every objection.

20

She was too young to be away from home. "But I won't be among strangers—I'll be with Blossom."

She couldn't give up school. "But I won't have to give up school. I can go on in New York. Mr. Wayburn will make arrangements with the principal so that I can be excused for a matinee on Wednesday."

Her music—she must not sacrifice that either. "Oh no, indeed! There is a piano backstage and I can practice there just the same as if I were right at home!"

Daniel MacDonald was probably too concerned with earning a proper living to object strenuously to Jeanette's accepting the job with Wayburn. He left it to Mrs. MacDonald, who later remembered, "I didn't want to be a foolish mother and stand in her way—maybe this was an opportunity."

Thus Jeanette was on Broadway in the *Demi Tasse Revue*. Wayburn continually devised skits which featured Jeanette as the butt of jokes. The young performer may not have been too excited at this ironic transformation and perhaps thought less of Wayburn because of it. But Wayburn was also unpopular with a man who would later become famous as Major Bowes, the radio personality, then owner of the theater. They had a violent disagreement over business matters and the *Demi Tasse Revue* was closed down three weeks after it opened.

One source asserts that the MacDonald family moved into New York and "closed their Philadelphia home" only after the opening of the *Demi Tasse Revue* which employed Jeanette and Blossom. A better view might be that the family moved to the place where at least one child was gainfully employed. Whether Daniel found a position before or after Jeanette's short run with Wayburn is unknown. But the possibility of three steady jobs and a fresh start for the father must have seemed very inviting.

Having lost her first Broadway job, Jeanette was not content just to continue with high school and her dancing lessons with Albertina Rasch. The way the young and hopeful musical comedy star earned her next role is a tribute to the MacDonald tenacity. Making the rounds of offices in search of theatrical employment, she happened to make the headquarters of Charles Dillingham, a sharp, experienced Broadway producer, her next stop. After a series of frustrating rejections,

21

Jeanette was told by Dillingham's secretary that her employer was out of town. In fact, she was told, he was in Algiers.

Jeanette sat in the reception room, undaunted by the officious secretary. As one story has it, she eventually got tired of waiting and started to leave. In the outer office area, she noted a room which had the words "broom closet" written on the door. Thinking it rather strange such a posh suite of offices should have a lowly designation as a broom closet so near the central area, Jeanette decided to investigate. Turning the door knob and entering, she was faced with a very surprised producer named Dillingham sitting at his desk. The ruse to ward off scores of aspiring stars did not work on the girl with the stubborn streak of Scot in her.

Dillingham was impressed by her verve. After a brief talk and demonstration of her talents, he offered her a replacement role in the chorus of *The Night Boat,* then trying out in Rochester. The producer had received a frantic wire that morning, pleading for another girl, so Jeanette was a godsend.

Jeanette reached Buffalo to find, according to one version, that the part was no longer open. But she bothered all concerned to such an extent that they provided her with a chorus part. As players Hal Skelly, John H. Hazzard and Stella Hoban starred up front in the Jerome Kern musical, Jeanette was cavorting behind them, in the chorus. *The Night Boat* opened on Broadway on February 2, 1920, at the Liberty Theatre. By this time her part in the proceedings was a bit more imposing because one of the minor leads had tumbled down a flight of steps and broken her leg. Ambitious Jeanette, who knew all the main female parts, was a natural for the role.

If some in later years would consider Jeanette too prim and proper, such was definitely *not* the case in 1920. In fact, one of Dillingham's co-workers took an intense interest in the young player. He worked with her extensively on play rehearsals and singing lessons. One evening he made the inevitable pass at her. Of course, she rebuffed him, and, as the account is told, he was removed from *The Night Boat* production and did not work for eight months.

The Night Boat enjoyed a run of 148 performances and then it was time for Jeanette to seek new employment. In the theater world of 1920 this was not overly difficult. That year 157 plays were produced, averaging a new opening every other day. The typical play made a

22

healthy if not spectacular ninety-eight-performance stand. Holdovers from the prior season included *Lightnin'*, *The Gold Diggers*, and *Irene*, all lighthearted romps. In the first year of The Roaring Twenties, Broadway was mostly, if not all, singing and dancing. Nothing could have been more opportune for Jeanette.

In the latter half of 1920 Jeanette landed a small part in *Irene*. She played Eleanor in the play's Chicago run. It was her biggest and longest engagement to date. Aside from the obvious good cheer brought on by another step up the professional ladder, she was able to continue to study singing and dancing. Feeling that a knowledge of foreign languages was necessary to the well-trained singer, Jeanette enrolled in the Berlitz School of Languages and studied French and later Spanish. She learned to speak each tongue flawlessly.

After the almost-affair with the rogue associated with the Dillingham office, Jeanette was a bit wary of show-business males. It is said she carried her huge cotton umbrella to interviews even on the sunniest of days, and when she returned to New York from Chicago took her father up on his constant suggestion that he escort her from the theater of any show after the performance.

In September, 1921, she replaced Martna Lorber as "Kate Allen" in the musical comedy *Tangerine* at the Casino Theatre in New York. Joseph Herbert, Jr., Harry Puck, and Billy Rhodes were her co-stars. The production, which had opened in early August that year, ran for 337 performances. Jeanette would not accompany the troupe on tour because she could not bring her mother along. By this time her normally tight attachment to her mother's apron strings must have been welded even tighter in trying to escape the grasp of backstage Lotharios.

The next year on Broadway was a bit different in tenor from the preceding ones. Nudging the domination of musical comedies was a series of Shakespearean revivals that caused the season to be the first in recent memory not described as the "worst in years." Among the more distinguished entries were John Barrymore's *Hamlet* and sister Ethel's *Romeo and Juliet*.

Shakespearean drama was not exactly Jeanette's forte, but the professional breaks still fell her way. Going up in an elevator one day, she noticed a little middle-aged man staring intensely at her. She was on the way to see her agent Max Hart in the Loew's State Theatre

Building. The enigmatic man asked—seemingly out of the blue—"Do you sing?" Suspicious, but always in the mood to make another job connection, Jeanette replied, "Yes." He asked her name. She told him.

The questions kept coming and Jeanette, usually full of high spirits, was amused, rather than angered. As the elevator reached her floor, she got out, followed by the short gentleman. He called to her, and handed her his calling card which read, "J. Baldwin Sloan." Not recognizing the name, she did not know how to respond. He was undaunted, explaining that he was a Greenwich Village producer looking for someone to replace the lead in his new production. The original girl came from Kansas City and was unsuitable for the demanding part. Oddly enough (perhaps a publicist's later embellishment), Sloan's lawyer was situated on the same floor as Max Hart. Almost convinced but still cautious, Jeanette made Sloan bring the noble barrister into the hallway to discuss a deal, apparently having learned that locked or closed doors often unleash the beast in men.

The play, a musical comedy of course, opened in Greenwich Village in September, 1922. It was considered little more than an amateur production, but Jeanette won a lead role for the first time. She scored a personal triumph singing a song called "I've Got the Blues," a torch number quite unlike the arias she studied. And Jeanette was still clinging to her original ambition, "imbued with the idea that singing in concert, in recital was the ultimate goal. . . . It seems to me in the music world it is the dearest challenge . . . you are all by yourself with only a piano accompaniment . . . you are out there on your own."

While Jeanette was between jobs early in 1922, her future partner Nelson Eddy was, in January of that year, making his debut, albeit unbilled, as the King of Greece in a show called *The Marriage Tax* in Philadelphia. The show was backed by non-show-business people, and the reporters who reviewed the show, many of them Eddy's personal friends from his newspaper days, saw it as a social event rather than a work of art. Later that year, in May, Eddy won the role of Strephon in *Iolanthe*, in competition with one hundred other male singers. *Iolanthe* played at the Broad Street Theatre in Philadelphia. One can only wonder whether Jeanette ever returned to her home town during those busy years, and whether perhaps she attended one of Eddy's performances.

Back in New York, Jeanette was building her stage reputation in

24

the cast of *Fantastic Fricassee,* that Greenwich Village revue which would run for 112 performances. Attending the show one night were people who would provide Jeanette with yet another boost to the stardom she wanted so desperately. Playwright Zelda Sears and her husband Louis Wiswell, general manager for producer Henry W. Savage, saw Jeanette perform, and liked her footlight charm. Even before *Fantastic Fricassee* had run its course, Jeanette was offered an ingenue role in *The Magic Ring.* Others in the cast were Mitzi (Hoag), Boyd Marshall, and that hulking gem of a performer, Sydney Greenstreet.

In an advertisement for *The Magic Ring* which opened at the Liberty Theatre on West 42nd Street on October 1, 1923, Jeanette was described as "the girl with gold-red hair and sea-green eyes." The imaginative label clung to her for quite a few years. So, in 1923, Jeanette became a Broadway starlet as Iris Bellamy cavorting through a prologue and three acts. Unfortunately for the play and its players, the season on Broadway was crammed with fine drama, and *The Magic Ring* was consequently only mildly successful, lasting ninety-six performances. Among the distinguished dramatic offerings were Sutton-Vane's *Outward Bound,* George Kaufman and Marc Connelly's *Beggar on Horseback* and Lula Vollmer's *Sun Up.*

One of the earlier tales of Jeanette's audition for Ned Wayburn for the *Demi Tasse Revue* has also been ascribed to her tryout for Henry W. Savage. One version has it that Jeanette was extremely nervous at the time and, while singing to a piano accompaniment, her voice cracked attempting to capture a very high note. He asked her to dance. She fell on her face. Yet she earned the part. It seems improbable that a seasoned producer like Savage would cast a girl who offered such an unstellar audition, but they say show people have special intuition. . . .

By the time of *The Magic Ring,* Jeanette was earning from $250 to $300 weekly, a very healthy salary in that day. As a brightening Broadway denizen, it was natural for her to attract male admirers. For the most part, she shirked romance—especially making the rounds of the speakeasy clubs that populated Prohibition-deluged Manhattan— and concentrated on her career, which had come to mean almost everything to the maturing young woman.

But romance was to come one night at the Beaux Arts Ball in New York. Jeanette was finally taking some time off evenings from her secret voice lessons with Grace Adele Newell (she was gaining a reputation as a dancer and wanted recognition as a singer, too). One of her friends arranged a date for Jeanette, so a foursome went to the extravagant ball in search of diversion. Jeanette later recounted her memory of her escort:

> As it turned out, he wasn't at all the sort of person I would have selected for myself. I think he found my lack of interest definitely dampening to his intention of having a very gay time indeed. Anyway, he decided I wasn't to interfere with his evening's enjoyment and after our first dance he muttered a vague excuse and wandered, not only away, but out of my life.

But the momentous evening was far from over. As she related it,

> Clad in my 1880 costume, all beruffled and becurled, I sat against the wall. Here I was, at the brilliant Beaux Arts Ball, to which I had looked forward so eagerly, a wallflower! In the midst of that gay throng of people intent upon the pursuit of pleasure, I sat soberly surveying the scene—an outsider. It never occurred to me to fortify myself with a visit to the punch bowl, even though everyone I saw rather obviously had done so. Truly, I felt more alone than I've ever felt in my life.

Fate was to intercede.

> Just as I decided to go home, a familiar face appeared; a charming man I had met casually, a doctor, came up and asked me to dance. Before we had got more than a few steps, however, a man tapped the doctor on the arm and said he was cutting in. The doctor introduced him to me and as we danced away, called: "Take care of her, Thorn."

Thorn was her first real romance since Raymond Scott, fifteen years earlier.

My new partner was tall, blond and handsome, just about the handsomest man I've ever seen. . . .

One can only wonder if he resembled a tall, blond, handsome man named Gene Raymond, or, for that matter, Nelson Eddy.

A divine dancer, too. My evening was saved. He was very protective of me, not allowing any of the men to cut in. I liked him, liked the fact that he hadn't visited the punch bowl either. We laughed at our finding each other in that great gaiety-pursuing crowd. Laughed at the swirling mob and laughed because we both knew that we would see each other again and again. You know how you know things—like that?

He took me home, and I said "yes" when he asked to call the following day. So started our romance, a romance that should have ended in marriage. But it was not destined to end that way, I guess.

Thorn was a student at New York University, and was very surprised to discover that Jeanette was an actress. Presumably the typical college man's idea of a performer, a female one anyway, was as "loose" as the woman at whom he was making a pass. The young man was an architecture student, and in many ways not typically collegiate, despite his misconception about pure Jeanette. It might be added the misconception was a happy one on his part.

From his father's allowance, Thorn purchased a snappy roadster automobile, but his clothes were tailored by the conservative Brooks Brothers. Not a raccoon hair could be found on the car seats. The couple dated frequently, and on chilly Saturday afternoons when he and the showless Jeanette attended football games, Thorn's typically collegiate flask was really a thermos filled with hot coffee.

The much-in-loves planned on marriage, but had to wait. Innumerable obstacles clouded their path. None of the barriers were serious, but surmounting all of them proved impossible eventually. First Thorn had to finish school at N.Y.U. Then he had to assume a post with his father's firm until he could establish himself as an independent architect and support Jeanette in the proper manner.

27

It was after *The Magic Ring* closed that Thorn courted Jeanette. For the next year she was out of work, except for a few assignments modeling fur coats. She later explained, "There didn't seem to be any place on Broadway for redheads." She earned good wages as a model, but having to wear bulky fur coats in mid-July and smile proved too much. So she deserted what had become a lucrative modeling career to try to find another show.

While Jeanette was floundering artistically, if not romantically and financially, in New York, Nelson Eddy was professionally progressing in Philadelphia. Alexander Smallens, the conductor of the Philadelphia Civic Opera Company, took a specific interest in Nelson's career. This resulted in Eddy's opening with the company that year as Amonasro in *Aida*. During the course of the show, he also mastered an impressive range of roles in the company's repertory.

As with other portions of Jeanette MacDonald's early life, it is unclear exactly when her romance with Thorn terminated. Some say it lasted until after her father's death in late 1924, others insist they broke up around the time of his demise. Yet another source alleges she was away from Thorn for one year—on the road in a show—and came back to New York because Daniel MacDonald was dying.

By this time Jeanette, who never graduated from high school, had achieved a stardom of sorts. She was usually cast as the leading dancer in a show, but yearned to display a long-cultivated singing voice. At least she had the dream of her eventual marriage to Thorn to console her.

> Other girls had more fun, lots of masculine attention, but they had lots of heartaches too! I cherished the thought of Thorn. I was proud of our love, faithful to our promise to be true to each other even though circumstances kept us apart. I was desperately lonely, yet I did not even want to go out with anyone else, and never did. My mother accompanied me on all my tours and I spent my time away from the theater in study.

The 1924–1925 Broadway season was considered a revival year. Unfortunately, the plays being rehashed had nothing to offer the specific talents of Jeanette MacDonald. Among the productions were

Voltaire's *Candide*, Ibsen's *The Wild Duck*, Molnar's *The Guardsman* (ironically, a quarter of a century later she would tour in it with husband Gene Raymond), and Congreve's *Love for Love* and *The Way of the World*. But Twenties' Broadway producers saw Jeanette only as a dancer. Her comedic talents, displayed early on in the *Demi Tasse Revue*, and occasionally in her feature films, were for the most part, left dormant. She had enough of a battle trying to promote her glorious vocal tones to fight for sophisticated comedy parts. And she wanted to sing publicly so desperately.

She was finally offered a role in *Tip-Toes*, produced by Alexander Aarons and Vinton Freedley. On December 28, 1925, the show opened at the Liberty Theatre with music and lyrics by the Gershwins (George's melodies, Ira's words). Others in the cast were Robert Halliday, Amy Revere and Allen Kearns. Jeanette's salary as a dancer rose to $350 per week. It helped to justify the expense of her new bachelor digs on West 55th Street and to support her mother now that Mr. MacDonald was dead. Most pressing, however, was her toppling romance with Thorn.

For some reason, Jeanette and Thorn severed their relationship in a hotel lobby! Both realized the romance was over; the gulfs between their professional and personal needs were too great. From all reports, when the couple parted company it was the last time they ever saw one another.

After the 194 performances of *Tip-Toes*, Jeanette decided to be firm with herself. She sublimated her emotional heartache by studying harder than ever—if that was possible—and by going to evening lectures, often on philosophy. Usually her mother accompanied her. At this point in her career, Jeanette determined not to accept any more dancing roles. She would sing on stage or do nothing. For a time the latter course held sway. Abandoning a lucrative income as a dancer was a courageous move and for a spell she paid for her bravery by constant unemployment, broken by occasional mannequin assignments.

In mid-1926 Jeanette's sister Blossom married Warren "Clarence" Rock (who remained her spouse until his death in 1960). In August of that year, Jeanette journeyed to Philadelphia to appear in the Broadway-bound *Bubbling Over*, backed by a group of wealthy Pennsylvanians. The show opened at the Garrick Theatre in Philadelphia in August, but lasted only two weeks. Despite the show's failure it was a sufficient showcase to provide the impetus for her being hired for the prima donna role in the Chicago run of *Yes, Yes, Yvette*.

The show, with lyrics by Irving Caesar and music by Phil Charig and Ben Jerome, had tremendous success in Chicago, and later in Boston and Philadelphia. The producer, H. H. Frazee, was so impressed with the popularity of *Yes, Yes Yvette* (apparently the response to the 1924 Broadway hit, *No, No, Nanette*) and its new prima donna, Jeanette MacDonald, that he decided to bring the venture to New York. Triumph at last! As Jeanette recalled it:

> When I arrived backstage for the Christmas Eve show, the entire cast was waiting to tell me the good news. The producer had decided to put my name in lights and star me, as a sort of Christmas present. I tried to be blasé in the face of their tingling emotion. I think I smiled and said, 'Isn't that nice?' As soon as possible, though, I slipped out the stage entrance, hired a taxi and began circling the block. Each time I passed the theater I looked back to see my name in lights. As I saw my name twinkling in the night, do you know my greatest thrill? A friend of the family's, Arnold Daly, had once advised me to shorten my name because it would never fit in the lights. But I had never been able to think of a shorter name. No other name seemed to suit me. And there it was! In lights—*all* of it. It wasn't too long. After about four trips around the block, I stopped at a drug store and called Mother about the good news and she and my sister came downtown to see the lights for themselves.

In New York, *Yes, Yes Yvette*, with Jeanette, Jack Whiting, Charles Winninger and Roland Woodruff, was not the hit promised by encouraging out-of-town runs. The show opened at the Sam H. Harris Theatre on October 3, 1927, but folded after forty performances. Yet *Yes, Yes Yvette* and especially Jeanette earned some rave reviews. In the *New York World*, Bide Dudley enthused, "Miss MacDonald is exquisite at all times, and she and Mr. Whiting supply the piece with a goodly share of its sunshine."

Having scored such a personal triumph in *Yes, Yes Yvette*, Jeanette was constantly being interviewed by the press. She was asked her opinion on almost every subject. Of course, she had numerous and enlightening comments to make on the state of men and women, together and separately.

On women:

> The motive of the woman today seems to be brisk efficiency in experiencing everything. She does not want to share a man's freedom; she wants a freedom of her own. But I cannot help feeling that woman is on the threshold of the realization that mere reckless "freedom" is the last thing in the world that will bring her happiness, or set her free from the persistent clamoring of her woman's soul for the things which nature has made stronger than herself—her instincts for wifehood and homemaking. I do not mean that women will suddenly relinquish the strides they have made in the commercial and artistic worlds. There will still be a goodly percentage of us who will find that Fate, or inclination, has placed us in a niche outside the home.
>
> The average, hectic young thing who has been unconsciously swept along an emotional epidemic for new sensations is already settling down today, if I am not mistaken, and her younger sister will, tomorrow, accept a more placid existence without question.
>
> Woman, like man, can only be free when she follows her finest and strongest instincts. To have these smothered because of the faddish frenzy of the moment is ludicrous.
>
> I am glad that my new role in this musical is that of a girl who places the love of the man she is going to marry above everything else. She is a type that is alluringly womanly and comfortably old-fashioned.

Obviously Jeanette was light years away from the devil-may-care flapper of the Twenties, the fun-crazed jazz baby as portrayed on screen by Joan Crawford or the rambunctious celluloid "It Girl" of Clara Bow. Instead, Jeanette was sensibly and determinedly formulating the blueprint for her life, a scheme that would extend a decade past the time of her comments now. Having endured years of intensive search for self-expression and success as a singer, she is telling the public that woman's "instinct" for wifehood and homemaking will emerge eventu-

31

ally. And this is exactly what would happen to Jeanette, or perhaps what she *made* happen.

Attuned to the necessity of promoting *Yes, Yes Yvette*, Jeanette also interwove advertisements for the show into her open forum discussions. A newspaper article of the time stated that "if she ever marries it will be none but an American. The home product, she protests, is good enough for her." According to the reporter, Miss MacDonald admired the character of Bob Bennett, the romantic hero of *Yes, Yes Yvette,* because he

> . . . has lots of pep, a sense of humor and sufficient initiative and confidence in himself to undertake seriously even such a farcical wager as that upon which revolves the plot of *Yes, Yes Yvette*—to tell nothing but the truth for five hours. Only an American would have the cool nerve to run the risk of appearing utterly ridiculous in order to prove something he believed in sincerely.
>
> Then again, American men are the most chivalrous in the world. They may not be as polished as the French, or as outwardly courteous as the English; but in their hearts they have the greatest admiration and respect for womankind. They show it in practical care and financial protection they afford their wives, sweethearts and sisters.
>
> When an American is in love, he wants to lay his entire fortune at her feet. Nothing seems too difficult to accomplish when it comes to making her happy. Like the hero in *Yes, Yes, Yvette,* he might even be willing to tell nothing but the truth for five consecutive hours, and that is going some for any man.

Life was not all work for Jeanette. She was a jubilant optimist and derived pleasure from the simplest lark, whether shopping for clothes, surprising her mother with a special gift, or dining with friends. She loved to recall the time when she and Emily West (a musical comedy aspirant who later would become Jeanette's private secretary) dined at Mamma Leone's Italian Restaurant on West 48th Street and recklessly ate spaghetti with garlic sauce, unmindful of the telltale breath their co-workers would have to endure during the evening performance. For

32

the record, Jeanette was severely reprimanded by the producer and promised not to repeat that gustatorial stunt, at least on days when she was performing in front of the footlights.

Yet, had Jeanette been more daring—or frivolous, according to one's point of view—she might have speeded up the progress of her show-business success. Not only might she have taken a more active part in accompanying producers, backers, playwrights or composers on nights on the town, but she might have agreed to performing after hours at the vast array of showcasing speakeasies that dotted Broadway of the late Twenties. But Jeanette had her own rigid code.

Meanwhile, in the extravagant temper of 1928, Broadway was enjoying tremendous prosperity. Ethel Barrymore unveiled the new theater bearing her name with *The Kingdom of God,* Ina Claire bubbled in *Our Betters,* Lee Tracy blasted his way through *The Front Page* and Miss Mae West shone in her self-written *Diamond Lil.* Among the younger performers sparkling on the Broadway stage were Claudette Colbert, Fredric March, Miriam Hopkins, Phillips Holmes and Sylvia Sidney, all of whom, like Jeanette, would soon join the acting stable at Paramount Pictures.

Shortly after the close of *Yes, Yes, Yvette,* Jeanette was signed by producer Hassard Short to appear in *Sunny Days.* As Ginette Bertin, Jeanette played in *Sunny Days* from the opening night of February 8, 1928, until closing night 101 performances later. The show had had an earlier run under the aegis of the Shubert Brothers and had cost $5.50 per ticket. Hassard Short offered the same play with Jeanette for only $3.00. *Sunny Days* was formerly known as *The Kiss in a Taxi,* and many thought both titles nonsensical.

Jeanette's Ginette was a Parisian flapper employed in a flower shop who falls in love with an author and dismisses an older banker suitor called "lobster daddy." Everybody was involved in a series of charming mix-ups before the final wedding scene. E. F. Harkins of the *Boston Advertiser* was complimentary toward the musical comedy. "*Sunny Days* is a capital farce comedy sprinkled with songs and dances. It has some of the snappiest lines dispensed from any Hub stage in a long time." Of the songs, Harkins found the comedy ones best, and reported that Jeanette "is a charming blonde who sings and dances expertly and looks better in lingerie—these Paris flower girls change their clothes every time they make a sale—than most prima donnas

33

would, you can bet." *Sunny Days* was also notable for being the final appearance of a then famous comedian, Billy B. Van, who, Harkins insisted, "was never better."

Following *Sunny Days*, Jake Shubert signed Jeanette for a musical comedy based on Captain Robert Marshall's novel, *The Royal Family*. Under the title *The Queen's Taste*, it previewed in Philadelphia in November, 1928, and the following month debuted on Broadway as *Angela*. Eric Blore and Alison Skipworth were the co-stars. The production lasted a brief forty performances.

However, the failure of *Angela* was something of a personal victory for Jeanette. First, she had the opportunity to play a princess, thus fulfilling one of her childhood dreams. As Princess Alestine Victorine Angela, daughter of King Louis VII and Queen Ferdinande, Jeanette cavorted in regal robes and gowns the way she had always desired.

More importantly, celebrated stage and Paramount film actor Richard Dix was in the audience of *Angela* one evening. He may have attended to consider Jeanette for his new feature film, a talkie to be called *Nothing But the Truth*. Dix, always seeking and fostering fresh talent, was impressed by Jeanette, and arranged for her to make a screen test at Paramount's Astoria Studio on Long Island.

Opinions vary as to the quality of the screen test. Some say crude sound equipment and flat cinematography harmed Jeanette's audition. Whatever the success or failure of the test, Jeanette was not to appear with Dix in *Nothing But the Truth*. (Helen Kane and Wynne Gibson were eventually selected.) The Shubert Brothers would not release Jeanette from her stage contract, or even allow her to appear for filmmaking during the day. Presumably the producers recognized the precarious position of *Angela*, and decided it was best if Jeanette posited all her energies in their faltering show.

While Jeanette was wavering between film and theater in Manhattan, Nelson Eddy decided that a change of focus was necessary for his career's well-being. Believing a concert engagement would garnish more attention than appearing in shows, Nelson arranged for a debut in Philadelphia. Shortly thereafter he went on tour "hoping for $50 a concert and glad to get $25." For the tour, he enlarged his repertory to nearly 500 songs and hired an accompanist, Theodore Paxson, who remained with him for almost forty years.

Despite the early closing of *Angela*, Jeanette was more confident than ever and started relaxing a bit, even attending social functions. At a Mayfair party she was seated at a table with her escort, when the couple was interrupted by a tall, good-looking friend of her date's. He was introduced as "Mr. Hemingway," and asked Jeanette to dance. While they were on the dance floor he requested her phone number. She gave it to him, but he did not bother to write it down. Jeanette thought the man was just being polite.

The next day the polite man telephoned Jeanette, asking for a luncheon date. She said no. After several further refusals to similar proposals, she finally consented, impressed with his persistence.

If it can be believed, Jeanette and "Mr. Hemingway" dated for two months without either realizing the other's true identity. Jeanette believed "Mr. Hemingway" was indeed Mr. Hemingway, while the man in question thought the woman introduced as Jeanette Mac-Donald was playing an elaborate hoax. Then one evening, after a performance of *Angela,* Jeanette was surprised to find "Mr. Hemingway" waiting in her dressing room. After at least a half dozen subsequent dates, she discovered that her beau was Bob Ritchie, a well-to-do New York stockbroker. He in turn discovered Jeanette was exactly who she said she was.

Jeanette and Ritchie were constant companions for several years. It can be surmised that she was always too concerned about her career to get really serious about marriage, and possibly still felt the scars of the break with Thorn. In any event, Ritchie later abandoned his Wall Street career to become Jeanette's business manager. If he could not be her husband, he could at least be in her life in a business way.

While her rollicking romance with Ritchie continued on its seesawing course, Jeanette agreed to perform in another Shubert musical comedy, *Boom Boom.* Perhaps the one distinguishing feature of the show was the cute-as-pie advertising campaign for the production. A prominent ad displayed a sketch of a showgirl sitting on the floor smarting with pain, with the print above reading, "I faw down and go *Boom Boom.* "

The ad proved prophetic. The show lasted a brief seventy-two performances, after debuting at the Casino Theatre on January 28, 1929. *Boom Boom,* a two-act musical comedy about a young woman named Jean (Jeanette) who weds an older man but really loves his son Tony, did, however, garner some pleasant reviews. Alvin J. Kayton of

35

the *Brooklyn Citizen* wrote, "As a whole, *Boom Boom* manages to provide a lively enough evening." Of course, he liked Jeanette, adding, "Jeanette MacDonald and Stanley Ridges played the respective roles of Jean and Tony more than well." Another member of the cast was Britisher Archie Leach who would gain prominence a few years later in Paramount films as Cary Grant.

One of the reasons Jeanette enjoyed performing in *Boom Boom* so much was, as she said, "there was none of that 'temperamental backstage conflict' that usually goes on at shows among people trying to undermine one another." Another reason young and winsome Jeanette liked the show's run was her friendship with Leach. Years later she would jokingly recall how tongue-tied he was with the opposite sex and how she tried to make him feel more welcome. A strong camaraderie developed between the two as "we became fast friends and remained so for years and years." They spent a good deal of time together, joking, and often going to lunches at Rudley's Restaurant across the street from the theater on 41st and Broadway. In fact, as it developed, both Jeanette and her co-player had their screen tests at Paramount at the same time, *but* separately.

Later Jeanette and the future Cary Grant met to compare notes. They both agreed it was "pure torture" and that what they had to do before the cameras "never had any sense or reason." For the life of them, they could not fathom why they had been asked to say meaningless lines or to "burst" into song and dance for equally "no reason." Of one thing they were certain, the auditions had been "dismal failures."

In Grant's case, his initial prognosis proved true. He was told he had "bow legs and his neck was too long." Eventually Hollywood would change its mind about this Britisher. As for Jeanette, in a matter of months the pieces of her professional life would fall into place better than ever.

CHAPTER THREE

While Jeanette was on the road playing in the Chicago run of *Boom Boom,* a stranger was taking great delight in watching her perform in New York. German director Ernst Lubitsch, a man famous for romantic historical films in Europe, had gained a greater reputation with sophisticated sex comedies in Hollywood. He took delight in viewing Jeanette's Paramount screen test for *Nothing But the Truth.* The audition footage had been shelved for a year and Lubitsch, in town to cast his latest feature and first talkie, *The Love Parade,* saw the rescued celluloid.

Lubitsch was elated. He enthused in his accented voice, "If this girl can sing, it would be a miracle!" In order to witness Jeanette in person, the director stopped off in Chicago. We will never know precisely what he thought of *Boom Boom,* but Jeanette was crowned with a contract to appear in Paramount's *The Love Parade* as proof of Lubitsch's confidence in her. An amiable settlement was reached with the Shuberts, who previously had refused to relinquish Jeanette's stage services for less than $75,000.

Since Blossom MacDonald was busily engaged on Broadway and sister Elsie had opened a dance school in Philadelphia, Jeanette was accompanied to Hollywood by her mother and later by Bob Ritchie. It was a propitious time for the stage actress to reach the capital of motion-picture production. Since talkies had come to stay with the proven success of Al Jolson's *The Jazz Singer,* the industry had undergone a tremendous revolution. Careers of players and film-makers had fallen by the wayside in the transformation from screen silence to sound. It was inevitable that the new medium would latch onto musicals as a money-making proposition and by 1929 Hollywood was awash with all-talking, all-dancing, all-singing extravaganzas. Luckily for Jeanette she began her motion picture tutelege under the supervision of an acknowledged genius, a master of technique and commercialism.

What was even more fortunate for Jeanette was that her leading man, the actual star of the film (she received only featured billing), was imported French stage celebrity Maurice Chevalier. At age forty-one, he was known worldwide for his jutting lower lip, an impish grin, his straw hat, and thanks to talkies, his entrancing accent. He had made his talking film debut in Paramount's *Innocents of Paris*, introducing the tune most associated with him, "Louise." He and the 1929 musical comedy were big hits, substantiating Paramount's faith in the high-priced performer.

Originally, Chevalier thought *Innocents of Paris* would be a one-picture deal, resulting in his triumphant return to the music halls of France. He was not excited about film-making and feared that he was too old to become a major, continuing success in the field. But a healthy Paramount contract assuaged his doubts and he was assigned to star in *The Love Parade*. When he was told of the project, Maurice balked. He was reluctant to star as a dapper officer in the army of a mythical kingdom, fearing himself too old for the focal role. One wonders if he was also upset at playing a romantic part with Jeanette, a fresh actress who was anywhere from twenty-two to twenty-six years of age, depending on what birthdate one cared to believe.

But Lubitsch would not have any Gallic temper tantrums. When faced with a worried star, the director retorted, "In that case he should stop acting like a twenty-one-year-old prima donna!" Thankfully, Lubitsch was a diplomat. He had gallery portraits made of Chevalier in his *Love Parade* costumes, and made the star rehearse all the songs he would be singing in the film. Furthermore, since the script was not yet completed, Lubitsch insisted Chevalier attend the story conferences and that the scenarists not exclude the nervous Frenchman from contributing ideas. What must have pleased Chevalier most about his contract with Paramount was being allowed to sit about for weeks before production began, collecting his impressive salary.

During her Broadway years, Jeanette frequently read the movie fan magazines and imagined the life in Hollywood. The girl who always wanted to be a princess must have watched the deluge of costumed screen romances in the Twenties with envy. Now her dreams were becoming vivid realities.

Lubitsch's greatest concern about Jeanette's film debut was that she would appear too thin on camera. Ordering a prop boy to keep an eye on her on the set of *The Love Parade*, Lubitsch required her "guardian" to slip a malted milkshake into her hands every time she was idle. In the course of production, Jeanette would gain fifteen pounds. Even when she got home in the evening, the "Lubitsch touch" was evident. Mrs. MacDonald would cook a heavy dinner for her daughter, then put her to bed.

Jeanette MacDonald's life during the filming of *The Love Parade* had little of the pomp, pageantry and romance she had come to expect from the movie magazines and from the films themselves. She knew no one in Hollywood and Lubitsch's schedule did not leave much free time for socializing. Not surprisingly, social cliques were generally closed to the new stars, who posed a very real threat to the bastions of the silent film. But there was one actress who treated the lonely young woman with the cordiality she had expected from everyone. Paramount's top star, Clara Bow, made friendly overtures to Jeanette when they were introduced. The two women lunched together, and Clara gave her "rival" many tips on how to get along in Hollywood. Sadly the Jeanette MacDonalds of the time hurt immeasurably stars like Clara Bow; players who could and did give impressive performances in talking films, but who were outshone by newer personalities.

One studio contract player who was not overjoyed by Jeanette's arrival was young, bouncy Lillian Roth, who had earned her fame in the tough field of vaudeville and who years later would become famous for her bittersweet autobiography, *I'll Cry Tomorrow*. As Lillian recalls it,

> Mr. Lubitsch greeted me with a smile when I arrived on the set. There, before my awestruck gaze, was Maurice Chevalier, the beautiful Jeanette MacDonald, and a little man with expressive, merry eyes, Lupino Lane, a British actor.
>
> Mr. Lubitsch introduced me. "Do you remember me?"

39

I ventured to ask Chevalier. "I worked with you in the *Frol-ics.*"

He flashed his inimitable smile. "Of course—I remember—how could I forget?" Lubitsch passed out copies of the script. "Now, will you please sit there, Mr. Chevalier." He pointed to a bench. "And Miss MacDonald—" He stopped. Script in hand, I was floating ecstatically toward Chevalier's bench.

"No, Miss Roth. I want you to sit on the other bench with Mr. Lane. You're playing opposite him."

I was crestfallen. How naive could I have been? Who else but lovely Jeanette MacDonald would play opposite Chevalier? And I—and Mr. Lane—what were we to do?

I soon found out.

"We have two identical sets here," Lubitsch explained. "Mr. Chevalier and Miss MacDonald will sit on that bench. You, Miss Roth, will sit with Mr. Lane on this bench. He is Mr. Chevalier's butler. You are playing maid to Miss Mac-Donald's princess. They are having a love affair; you and Mr. Lane are having one, too. You two are to parody everything your master and mistress do. When they kiss, you kiss. When Mr. Chevalier declares his love for Miss MacDonald, Mr. Lane will declare his love for you. Get it?"

I got it. As Chevalier pursued Jeanette, at a high point in the scene, Lupino was to pursue me, bringing his face so close to mine that I was to gaze cross-eyed with love at him.

I had to hold tears back as Lubitsch sketched the ridiculous role I was to play. But I went through my lines.

And so with fears, jealousies and nervousness, *The Love Parade* went into actual production. On the set Jeanette was indeed a queen. Specifically, she played Queen Louise to Maurice Chevalier's Count Alfred, the rebellious playboy she marries early on in the film. In the picture, Jeanette wears a lovely court gown with a sweeping train of white satin that required two weeks for ten beadworkers to complete with the necessary stitching of sequins, rhinestones and pearls into the smooth fabric.

Even though Jeanette was the Queen in *The Love Parade,*

Lubitsch would often offset the regal glamour with riotous gyrations while modeling actresses' costumes to make sure they were just right. Jeanette's wardrobe was carefully supervised by him, and since Lubitsch was (believe it or not) allergic to zippers, the women had to be buttoned into their costumes. It is interesting to note in *The Love Parade* a feature that was to become a staple of Jeanette's Paramount films. Amidst the splendor of the pleasure palaces would be at least one sequence in which she would virtually model skimpy lingerie. One scene here had the modest Jeanette rising from her bed to be led to the bath in a revealing negligee, while singing "Dream Lover" (which she was soon to record).

With all of Lubitsch's precision and demands, his great sense of humor was a saving grace. It endeared him to the actress from the start. They had something of a playful relationship, although it was easy to discern the teacher from the student. Lubitsch once said of Jeanette, "She was very, very pretty and knew it . . . but she was underdeveloped within."

The light and serious sides of their professional rapport blended to keep things moving, and to maintain tempers at a workable level. At first, Lubitsch referred to Jeanette as "Mac." She did not care for that and threatened to call him "Lu." That quieted him, but devil that he was, the Continental Master designated his rising star "Donald." Jeanette blackmailed him by coming up with "Itsch," and that ended the spate of name-calling (at least for a spell). Actually Jeanette preferred to be called by her first name with friends and Miss MacDonald by acquaintances.

Lubitsch had a few names for Jeanette's entourage. Whenever Mrs. MacDonald was not on the set, Jeanette's singing teacher Grace Newell was on hand. The director called her Jeanette's "morals teacher." It was a marvel to the European that even when none of her supervisors were about, she never took a drink or smoked, and that she always worried that the scenes in underwear were a "little too much."

That became a frequent dialogue on the set.

JEANETTE: Isn't that a little too much?

LUBITSCH: You're not little Jeanette now. You're all grown up and my Queen! Be my Queen!

Years later, thinking back to the early Paramount films, Jeanette would reflect how admirable her mother had been never to comment directly about those risqué bedroom scenes. "I guess she knew me. . . . After all, as she used to say, it was what was inside a person that counted. She knew I was not like the characters I played." In fact, Jeanette was always very proud of her closely knit family, pointing out how each one was very individualistic and that each had a wonderful sense of humor.

Aside from lingerie modeling, Lubitsch enlivened the set of *The Love Parade* by his gymnastics with the camera. At one point in the production, both the script and score required the staging of two song duos at once. Lubitsch craftily devised a way to accomplish the feat with the still primitive sound film equipment. He set himself up on a milk stool between two bulky camera booths. Lillian Roth and Lupino Lane sat on a bench in an outdoor set, while Jeanette and Maurice Chevalier lounged in typically regal splendor inside the palace locale. Lubitsch then conducted the whole affair, and kept an eye on the orchestra, as the four sang expressively for the cameras. Having both sets adjacent to one another, of course, made it easier. Off to the left were the studio musicians, and microphones were suspended on cords over the heads of the players.

This kind of jovial but very professional nonsense decorated the set of *The Love Parade*. Lubitsch's efforts to bring out Jeanette's naturally alluring personality and sense of humor resulted in *The Love Parade*'s being one of the big hits of the 1929 film season. Everyone granted that the marriage of convenience between the lonely Queen of Sylvania and her errant foreign emissary, Count Alfred (Chevalier), was the most confectionary of plots, but it was handled with sophistication and abounding wit. There was a balance of Continental charm (provided by Chevalier), American allure (Jeanette's contribution), near slapstick farce (Lane and Roth's departments—with a delightful cameo assist from Ben Turpin as a cross-eyed servant), and a mixture of tempo-alternating songs (composed by Victor Schertzinger and Clifford Gray).

On Tuesday, November 19, 1929, *The Love Parade* had a charity premiere at the Criterion Theatre in New York City, with most of the principals from the film in attendance. The one major absentee was Maurice Chevalier, who had sustained a hand injury while working on another Paramount film, *The Big Pond* with Claudette Colbert. Instead, he recorded a message for the screen. A nervous Jeanette made

42

a short speech, and her mother and sisters were proud that the youngest member of the MacDonald family had come so far.

Reviewers of *The Love Parade,* while focusing on the talents of Chevalier and Lubitsch, did not ignore Jeanette's contributions to the adult proceedings. The *New York Times'* Mordaunt Hall assessed that Jeanette sang "charmingly." Other critics reported an alluring contrast projected by the screen newcomer. Here was a leading lady who might appear frosty on the exterior, but was obviously romantically boiling within. It was an enticing contradiction and contrast which suave Lubitsch smartly maneuvered for the benefit of the film and for Jeanette's budding screen career. Chevalier, with good cause, received the lion's share of critical and public adulation. In fact, for the 1929 Academy Award sweepstakes, Maurice was nominated for his performances in *The Love Parade* and *The Big Pond.* (He lost the coveted award to England's George Arliss, who had made such a mark with *Disraeli.*)

Years later *Time* magazine prompted Jeanette to reminisce about the trend-setting *Love Parade,* and her life and times on this well-regarded motion picture.

When there were some visitors on the set, he [Lubitsch] would say, "Now Miss MacDonald, try to act for a change. Ach, but you are a dumb girl!" When I asked why he had engaged me for the role if I were so dumb he would say, "Ach, I was dumb too, that day." . . . I told him I wanted a finished print of *The Love Parade.* Every time I told Lubitsch he would tell me, "Don't be so anxious, I've cut most of your scenes out. There's plenty of you lying around on the floors."

More seriously, Jeanette would later reflect about Lubitsch and his famed "touch."

I had my earliest training in films with Lubitsch, in the days when he was a real boudoir diplomat. He could suggest more with a closed door than all the hay-rolling you see openly on the screen nowadays, and yet he never offended."

43

They got along famously. However, one time, Jeanette recalled:

>I had come late three days running. The last time I was
just five minutes behind time. But Mr. Lubitsch had finally
lost all patience and more temper. He was in a rage. "Who
do you think you are? Do you know who I am? You aren't
big enough to do this to me."
>
>The upshot was that I had hysterics and he stormed into
the front office—while a company waited an hour instead of
five minutes. But before noon we had made it up, and our
friendship and professional understanding were stronger than
ever.

Jeanette's penchant for tardiness would be a sore point on her film
sets for years. Mrs. MacDonald acceptingly told a California newspaper, "Jeanette's never on time." But she insisted it was her daughter's
only known bad habit.

There are those who would have disagreed with her. Perhaps a
better known personality fault, denied more vehemently, was Jeanette's
Irish temper (she was part Irish). It led her into trouble one day on the
Paramount lot. A studio employee stopped Jeanette in the hall, as she
was coming from a projection room where she had been listening to
playbacks. He informed her it would be necessary to work late that
evening. She acknowledged the information only slightly. Her mind
was more concerned with events that had transpired in the screening
room.

That night when someone told her for the first time—so she
thought—that she would have to return to the studio, she became
dramatically annoyed. Jeanette was so sure the extra work was being
heaped on her out of meanness on some executive's part. Yet the
employee swore he had told Jeanette of the late call earlier that day.
At first no one could determine who was lying. Finally the truth was
pieced together. Had Jeanette shown a little less flair for emotional
release, the admittedly minor incident would have been much easier
to overlook and to forget.

But this was the quality of her life at Paramount in the early years.
Under Lubitsch's direction, she learned much, but also had to cope
with a loneliness she did not associate with the vital Hollywood scene.

Bob Ritchie was still in New York. Thorn and any other beaus or dates she had ever had were long gone. There was only Jeanette and mama and Mr. Lubitsch.

Yet Paramount did its best to provide for its newest screen discovery. Having sent her and Mrs. MacDonald East for the lush premiere of *The Love Parade,* the studio allowed her to remain in her favorite city to catch up with the gossip along the rialto, to renew old friendships, to do special media promotion for the film and, of course, to see Bob Ritchie. But the film company was practical and while in New York arranged for Jeanette to make her first professional recordings. Accompanied by a small orchestra under the supervision of Nat Shilkret (who would later be with Jeanette at M-G-M), she sang into the Victor microphones "March of the Grenadiers" and "Dream Lover" from *The Love Parade,* and also the tune "The Revelers." It was the beginning of a relatively productive and ultimately distinguished recording career. (Actually when Jeanette was a small child, she had gone to the local park with her mother and while there started singing loud and clear, using a sandbox for a stage. A bewildered parkkeeper was so impressed with the child's use of her lungs, voice and general energy that he brought mother and child to his house so Jeanette could make a recording on one of the crude devices of the day.)

Following the Hollywood maxim, "If it works once, try it again," Paramount had cast Jeanette in another musical, this time a true operetta, *The Vagabond King.* It ranks as one of Jeanette's least favorite movie ventures. Since Ernst Lubitsch was busy elsewhere at the time, the studio assigned Ludwig Berger to direct the project. Singing matinee idol Dennis King was given the title role, and the studio decided to expand the film's budget by employing two-tone Technicolor for the costume drama about the life of the French rogue-poet François Villon. The supporting cast included Lillian Roth and Warner Oland, the latter to become famous as the screen's most impressive Charlie Chan.

Jeanette had her share of problems with Mr. King, a man who had not yet adapted to the more subtle techniques of screen histrionics. In one particular scene, where Jeanette sings the lovely "Only a Rose" (and she looked as radiant as the flower itself), King was concerned that all the camera attention was being focused on her. Even when she had medium shots or close-ups, he persisted in being included in the lens' eye. He would sway left or right, to or fro, doing whatever possible to catch a bit of the limelight. He only served to make himself look more ridiculous. The release print finds bits of his face (especially his nose) lunging into view on the right hand side of the screen, as Miss Mac-Donald is attempting to complete her vocal selection. (In later years Jeanette and Gene Raymond would refer to this as the "Only a Nose" scene.)

The advertisements for *The Vagabond King* naturally built up the noble history of the William H. Post–Brian Hooker–Rudolf Friml property, but did little to insure its popular success.

> It lives again!—the thundering throb of "Song of the Vaga-bonds," in the glorious golden voice of Dennis King, star of Paramount's all-color musical romance, *The Vagabond King*! Once the greatest triumph of the Broadway stage, now the supreme triumph of the talking, singing screen—Para-mount's New World Show. Blazing with gorgeous Tech-nicolor throughout . . . vibrant with stirring melodies . . . packed with thrills and adventure, excitement, romance. With Broadway's favorite romantic stars, Dennis King and Jeanette MacDonald in the leading roles, and a great cast.

Despite the publicity, *The Vagabond King* was mild stuff, elicit-ing some good responses, but generally falling on the deaf ears of the paying customers and critics who were tiring of the song-and-dance cycle. In the *New York Times,* Mordaunt Hall termed the effort "beau-tiful and quite stirring." But the praise carried a heavy lump. He also found it the victim of poor writing by Herman J. Mankiewicz (the man who would have such a controversial role in the creation of *Citizen Kane* a decade later). Hall blamed Mankiewicz for the slow pacing and awkward shifts from realistic to fluffy romantic scenes. And director Ludwig Berger received his share of criticism. "Berger . . . has not succeeded in eliciting from Miss MacDonald much in the way of acting, and her enunciation never gives the slightest suspicion of be-longing to the period." The *Times'* reviewer did admit, however, that Jeanette sang "charmingly," citing her "Only a Rose" as being one of the best numbers in the generally lackluster presentation.

On January 19, 1930, a few weeks before *The Vagabond King* met

AT AGE ELEVEN.

WITH MAURICE CHEVALIER
IN *THE LOVE PARADE* ('29).

In *SUNNY DAYS* ('28)
ON BROADWAY.

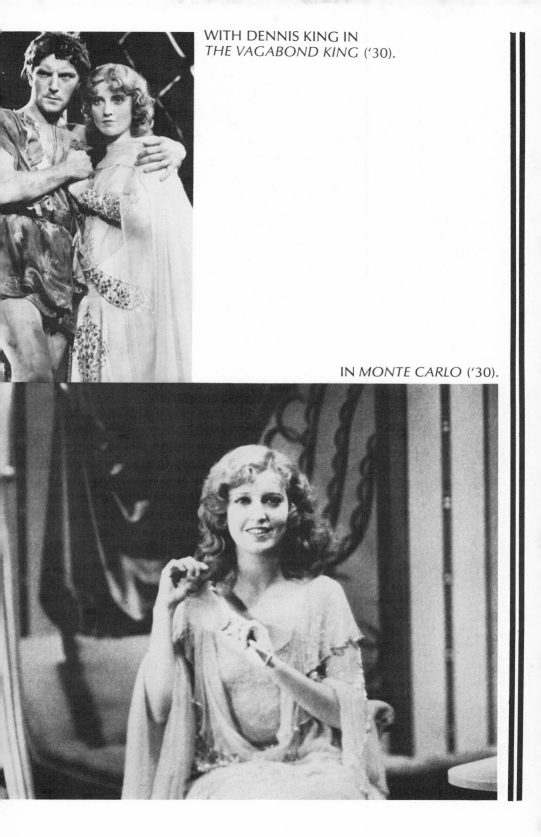

WITH DENNIS KING IN
THE VAGABOND KING ('30).

IN *MONTE CARLO* ('30).

WITH HER FAVORITE
DIRECTOR, ERNST LUBITSCH.

IN THE SPANISH
VERSION OF *PARAMOUNT
ON PARADE* ('30).

WITH HER MOTHER,
ANNA MACDONALD.

WITH SINGING
COACH
GRACE ADELE
NEWELL.

WITH
ZASU PITTS
AND JOE E. BROWN
IN *THE
LOTTERY BRIDE* ('30).

IN *OH, FOR A MAN* ('30).
WITH ALISON SKIPWORTH

WITH VICTOR MCLAGLEN
AND ROLAND YOUNG IN
ANNABELLE'S AFFAIRS ('31).

WITH ROLAND YOUNG IN
DON'T BET ON WOMEN ('31).

WITH BUSINESS
MANAGER
ROGER RITCHIE.

WITH MAURICE
CHEVALIER
IN *ONE HOUR
WITH YOU* ('32).

A MONTAGE OF SHOTS
FROM *LOVE ME TONIGHT* ('32).

with mixed commercial reaction, Jeanette journeyed out to Culver City, the home of M-G-M, to make another recording of "Dream Lover" for Victor Records. This version, with the orchestra under the supervision of Leroy Shield, was rejected by the phonograph record company as unsuitable for marketing. It was a professionally disappointing period for Miss MacDonald.

But in the strange way that business is conducted in California, Jeanette was experiencing a career rush in Hollywood. Paramount decided *Monte Carlo* should be her next starring vehicle, and that Ernst Lubitsch must supervise it. Meanwhile, United Artists was eager for Jeanette to sign a picture pact with them. Initially it was to be for one project, but later would be expanded to encompass other proposed properties. Since Jeanette did not have an official Hollywood business agent, she wired Bob Ritchie in New York to talk with top Paramount executive Jesse Lasky about the advisability of the United Artists deal. This would be Ritchie's first chance at managing show-business talent. Little did he suspect that his trip to Hollywood to close the deal would result in taking on Jeanette's business affairs, and handling those of other clients as well.

After Paramount underwent a period of self-analysis, it was agreed to chance showcasing Jeanette in *Monte Carlo* with "only" music and dancehall performer Jack Buchanan (a great favorite in his native England) as box-office insurance. It was a risk that production executive David O. Selznick fought against, but the studio had faith in Jeanette, or so it seemed.

Yet while she was busy on the soundstages in *Monte Carlo, Paramount on Parade* was released. This all-star revue contained sequences with most every contract player on the lot participating, from Iris Adrian and Richard Arlen to Stanley Smith and Fay Wray. Maurice Chevalier performed a slapstick sketch, "Origin of the Apaches," with Evelyn Brent and later in the proceedings was seen in a Technicolor song routine, singing "Sweeping the Clouds Away." Ernst Lubitsch directed both episodes. Where was Jeanette? Evidently with already 128 minutes of footage, it was decided to eliminate her scenes from the American release prints. But when the studio prepared its Spanish-language edition of the costly pastiche, Jeanette not only replaced Jack Oakie, Skeets Gallagher and Leon Errol as the Spanish-speaking mistress of ceremonies (with a perfect Castillian accent), but she had a vocal number set in a Venetian gondola. (Years later Jeanette and the Spanish-language *Galas de la Paramount* turned up in small art house theaters.)

"He's rich, he's wealthy, and he's got nothing but money!" says Jeanette's Countess Vera von Conti in *Monte Carlo* as she flees to the Riviera to escape marriage to a Duke. As she sits in a compartment of a moving train, peering out the window, she commences singing "Beyond the Blue Horizon," with the clever accompaniment of sounds of the locomotive's engine, wheels and whistle. Another interesting scene in the facile *Monte Carlo* has Jeanette and Buchanan (he playing Count Rudolph Fallieres) doing a duet over the telephone.

Leo Robin, Richard Whiting and W. Franke Harling composed the songs that propel *Monte Carlo* along its charming way, but it is the dialogue of Ernest Vajda and Vincent Lawrence that adds the chic spice to the plot. Yet, without the special care bestowed by Lubitsch, who can say if the repartee, the bons mots, the non sequiturs and the double entendres would have obtained the same joyous results. Jeanette was indeed fortunate to be again guided by Lubitsch at his peak.

Her final film for Paramount before shooting *The Lottery Bride* at United Artists was *Let's Go Native,* her fourth release in 1930. It was a young Leo McCarey who directed the zany, often incoherent *Let's Go Native,* a wild mélange that featured Jeanette, Kay Francis, Jack Oakie and Skeets Gallagher. The songs, including "I've Got a Yen for You" and "My Mad Moment," were the sanest things about this farce.

United Artists cannot be faulted with stinting on the production values of *The Lottery Bride,* released in November, 1930, with Technicolor sequences. Rudolf Friml and J. Keirn Brennan contributed the bulk of songs ("You're an Angel," "I'll Follow the Trail, "My Northern Light") to this original operetta, but the overall effect was vastly disappointing. Not that it was as disastrous as Grace Moore's M-G-M picture, *A Lady's Morals,* the story of Jenny Lind, but it was nowhere comparable to Jeanette's earlier Lubitsch offerings, or to, say, Lawrence Tibbett's *Rogue Song* at Metro.

The main distinguishing factor of *The Lottery Bride,* Jeanette's least favorite Hollywood motion picture, was that for the first time she received top billing. (Her co-players included John Garrick, Joe E. Brown, ZaSu Pitts and Carroll Nye.) Her singing was well received but

48

the plot was so incredible as to blur the already faint virtues of the feature. Jeanette played Jennie, a young girl who forces her boyfriend Chris (Garrick) into a three-day marathon dance, which concludes with the pair dropping from exhaustion. For some reason, Jennie enters herself in a "wife lottery." Chris apparently takes a ticket on Jennie and, not realizing he has won her, boards a dirigible headed for the Arctic Circle. The aircraft crashes, but somehow Jennie arrives way up north to be reunited with the husband who won her.

In between film and recording assignments, Jeanette found time to make her radio debut on NBC's "Camel Pleasure Hour" on November 19, 1930, exactly a year from the day her first film, *The Love Parade*, made its charity premiere in New York.

Toward the end of 1930, Jeanette had appeared in five films, yet her career had not really advanced much from *The Love Parade*. She filled out her schedule making recordings and radio offerings. However, without Lubitsch at the helm, it seemed she was destined to stagnate, at least at Paramount.

49

CHAPTER FOUR

Trends come and go in Hollywood. The musical comedy-operetta cycle had almost played itself to death by mid-1930. The public craved good, solid stories, not mock heroes and heroines cavorting on camera with a song on their lips and a tap dance on their feet. Each studio in turn realized the hazard of hanging onto a fading genre, and soon song-and-dance features were nearly *verboten.*

Jeanette's picture deal with Paramount had concluded and fearing an absence of offers if she waited too long, she allowed Bob Ritchie to negotiate a three-picture contract with Fox Films. By the time her first movie for that company was released in very late 1930, the screen musical was officially dead. To salvage the venture, *Oh, for a Man,* Fox snipped out most of the vocal numbers.

Yet there are some wry, delicious moments in the storyline. For example, at the opening of the feature, Jeanette appears as tempestuous opera singer Carlotta Manson. She is seen singing a Wagnerian aria, complete with long blonde wig and an appropriate costume. Suddenly the spotlight goes out—in the middle of her solo no less. She hisses, "the spotlight . . . the spotlight." After a curtain call, she walks off stage with eyes flashing, demanding "where is that son of an electrician?" After that the story tumbles downhill, as she converts a burglar (Reginald Denny) into a singer and then her groom.

Fox was enjoying a boom period with the vehicles of its screen love team, Janet Gaynor and Charles Farrell, and had little regard for the potentials of Jeanette MacDonald. It was decreed that there would be no more musicals for the transient from Paramount, and she was plopped into two fair-to-middling comedies, *Don't Bet on Women* and *Annabelle's Affairs*, both released in 1931.

If the public wanted froth, they certainly were dished out plenty in this chase-the-Depression-blues-away comedy. The story revolved around the brag by ungallant hero Edmund Lowe that he could kiss any girl in the space of forty-eight hours. Of course, Jeanette is the New York girl Lowe vows to oscillate. Perhaps the highlight of the heroine's appearances in this feature were her changes of wardrobe. Her garments included: 1) an accordion-pleated nightgown of chiffon lace with chiffon negligee (the skimpy drawers again!), with trimmed kimono sleeves; 2) sport dress of white crepe with godets inserted in the skirts, worn with a polka-dotted scarf; 3) a gold metal brocaded evening wrap with platinum fox trimming; 4) smart riding habit with tan silk blouse; 5) an evening gown of chiffon and lace ruffles and short train of lace, with a pearl necklace.

With a title like the one above, and a slight plot to boot, the advertising for *Don't Bet on Women* pursued a prurient tack. "One woman taught him all women were bad; another taught him he was all wet." "A maestro of love, he was merely a tyro in the hands of this woman who knew." "A woman's wiles against a man's technique—which would you bet on?" Apparently the audience and critics were not interested enough to gamble, and the feature, like Jeanette's other two Fox movies, is either lost or well hidden today.

Annabelle's Affairs did a better job of showcasing Jeanette's burgeoning comedic talents. The plot revolves around the on-again off-again romance between young Annabelle Leigh (Jeanette) and gruff miner John Rawson (Victor McLaglen). She marries the ore digger but later insists that he compromised her. Rawson heads West, leaving baffled Jeanette to seek employment as a cook at the estate of a Long Island playboy. Months later, a refined Rawson turns up—his mangy beard shaved off—and Annabelle falls in love with the gentleman, and they live happily ever after. There are some tangles between Annabelle and the millionaire over stock certificates, and this no doubt contributed to the craziness which lifted *Annabelle's Affairs* above her other Fox entries.

One of the more amusing on-set calamities of the semipedestrian *Annabelle's Affairs* goes as follows. The scene is set in the hallway of millionaire Roland Wimbledon's hotel room. Wimbledon (Roland Young) asks his butler (Sam Hardy) to whom he was just speaking. The butler answers his inebriated employer, "Mr. Wickham sir—the house detective." Wimbledon replies, "Inviting him down to my place to eat my wine and drink my food, I suppose." The whole set howled with laughter at the slip. Director Alfred Werker decided to keep the incorrect reading in, reasoning, "If it makes us laugh, it'll make the audience laugh."

Annabelle's Affairs received some nice reviews, among them from *Time* magazine, which had ignored the *nouveau* Jeanette in her first film, *The Love Parade*. *Time* seemed a bit surprised at the appearance of Jeanette's knack for comedy, and stated that her main filmic virtue to date had been "an aptitude for undressing before the camera quickly and almost completely with becoming grace and without embarrassment."

It is ironic that a woman many considered to be a bit too conservative (Maurice Chevalier later termed her a prude) was able to disrobe so casually before the eyes of the camera and the crew. The difference between Jeanette's early screen "morality" and her later conservatism can be attributed to the understanding that a young actress must do what is expected of her if she is to rise in the industry. So, Jeanette rolled with the punches until she achieved sufficient power to throw some of her own.

With her trio of Fox films behind her, there was little question that Winifred Sheehan, studio production executive, and Robert Ritchie would come to terms about additional projects to star Jeanette. The William Fox lot already had such marquee allures as Will Rogers, James Dunn, Warner Baxter, Joan Bennett, Spencer Tracy, the aforementioned Janet Gaynor and Charles Farrell, Elissa Landi, John Boles and Victor McLaglen.

Besides, Jeanette had more pressing problems. She was being sued by Mrs. Lucinda M. Reichenbach, widow of Harry L. Reichenbach, press agent. The plaintiff, in her $20,000 suit, charged that according to an agreement, Miss MacDonald had promised to pay her now deceased husband ten percent of her salary from September 1, 1929, to September 1, 1931, in return for publicity services. The suit was eventually settled out-of-court.

More importantly, Jeanette had to travel to Europe to reinstate

53

her overall career. How did this peculiar situation come about? As Jeanette would later outline it,

My picture *Monte Carlo* had been released in Europe. The atmosphere was so beautifully done that most Europeans thought we had made the picture in Monte Carlo instead of Hollywood. So, when a story broke in their newspapers concerning a certain crown prince and his clandestine love affair with a blonde girl, the rumor started that the girl was Jeanette MacDonald. The story was that the prince's wife caught her husband and his love together and shot the girl, who was taken to Italy. Whether she died or disappeared seems a mystery. At any rate, my pictures were immediately banned in certain sections of Europe.

Meanwhile, musical pictures suffered a setback in this country and I made three pictures for Fox in which I did no [sic] singing at all.

This caused the further report in Europe that I was not only dead but that my sister (who could not sing) had taken my place on the screen! This concerned me a great deal; musical pictures make money in Europe and I couldn't afford to lose this market by any such nonsense.

The only thing I could do was appear in concert in Europe and prove my identity with my voice. I arrived at Le Havre and officials were sent out to warn me about the antagonistic French press. Rumors had already reached the boat that I was to be barred from landing because I was merely there seeking publicity.

During four terrible hours of waiting, French news reporters hounded me with questions and because I understood but little (and answered in such garbled French) I presume I did myself more harm than good.

Finally we were allowed to land.

The crowd waiting on the docks was terrific and frightening. Perhaps their interest in me was the fact that I was rumored to be dead. But, at the moment, I thought nothing of their possible reasons for waiting to see me. I guess I thought I was getting my first taste of movie star celebrity.

I lost Mother and my secretary [and Robert Ritchie] between the boat and my car—and one shoe.

My first concert booking was the Empire. Everything was going smoothly until we got a warning of a possible demonstration against my performance. Obviously, there were still those who believed that fantastic story of my "romance" with a prince.

Of course, all concerned were shaken by the impending threat. The American Ambassador was away on a shooting trip in Scotland, so he could not be reached to calm the growing storm. The only advice the American Consulate could offer Jeanette was to obtain proof she had never set foot in Europe before September 4, 1931, the day of her recital at the Empire Theatre in Paris. She did.

An hour before curtain time, the manager of the theater had to cajole Jeanette into going on stage. The house was, quite naturally, sold out, and he did not want to make refunds. Plainclothesmen would be stationed strategically in the audience to prevent any attempted violence. Would she go on? Would she risk her life to entertain the paying guests? Yes!

As Jeanette glided onstage, the auditorium was silent. All eyes were on the young woman from Philadelphia. She proffered a brief smile. As soon as the audience recognized her goodwill, they burst into applause. Her first song brought a thunderous ovation, and the second, a French number, endeared Jeanette to the French forever. Jeanette MacDonald, who months, weeks, even hours earlier had been a villainess in Europe, was now the toast of Paris.

On the third night of her appearance at the Empire, Maurice Chevalier was in the audience. Invited to take a bow, the astute Frenchman instead trotted up to the stage, and Jeanette planted a kiss on his person. The papers, having exhausted the scandal about Jeanette's royal rendezvous, decided to create a romance between the pair. (Chevalier was then still wed to performer Yvonne Vallée.) In later years it became obvious Jeanette and Maurice had a professional respect for each other, but were *not* friends. The irony of it is understandable in retrospect, but back then it must have annoyed Jeanette, now the victim of gossip on two continents. Remember, she was also rumored engaged and/or married to Bob Ritchie at the time!

Later in September she crossed the English Channel to appear at the Dominion Theatre in London. On September 21, 1931, she debuted, and the town was here. The *London Times* reported:

> Fame comes more quickly through the medium of the screen than the variety stage, and Miss MacDonald had the assurance of a cordial welcome before the audience last night knew whether a voice and personality which had delighted two Continents would pass the severe test which a stage appearance imposes. Miss MacDonald herself was a little nervous about her ability to please, but the applause did not sag during her performance, and when, flushed with the appreciation of her most stirring film song, the "March of the Grenadiers" from *The Love Parade,* and with glinting hair falling in waves to her shoulders, she took a succession of final curtains, there could be no question of her success. It should be said for the theatre that she had all the advantages that skillful production could contribute. . . .
>
> Four of Miss MacDonald's songs were borrowed from the films in which she has played a prominent part, but in "Reviens" she showed quite prettily that she could be independent of what may be regarded as advance publicity.

Jeanette's *Monte Carlo* co-star, Britisher Jack Buchanan, hosted a fabulous party for her during her West End sojourn. That evening, the fans (called galleryites) had already formed their attachment to Jeanette MacDonald, and waited outside the hotel until the party ended to congratulate her.

Not ignoring her recording career, Jeanette recorded four of her repertory numbers at Small Queen's Hall in London on September 25. The songs were, "Dear, When I Met You," "Pardon, Madame," "Goodnight," and "Reviens" ("Return"). Back in Hollywood later that fall, Jeanette appeared on the NBC "Presidential Unemployment Program" on November 15, "The Fleishmann Hour" on December 4, and earlier in the year, another "Camel Pleasure Hour" on March 11, both on NBC network radio.

Jeanette did not forget the man largely responsible for starting the controversy about the fact and fiction of *Monte Carlo.* Andre Ranson,

French author of the scandalous novel, *Jeanette MacDonald,* was slapped with a lawsuit for stirring up trouble. The case was later settled out of court.

After the mild success in one of her Fox features, *Annabelle's Affairs,* and the notoriety she achieved abroad, Jeanette was suddenly considered very box-office worthy by Paramount Pictures. Ritchie negotiated a two-picture deal between the studio and Jeanette; she always abhorred long-term arrangements.

Since her last on camera liaison with Chevalier, he had made a trio of Paramount pictures, each in an English and a French-language edition: *The Big Pond* with Claudette Colbert (*La Grande Mer,* also with Miss Colbert); *Playboy of Paris* with Frances Dee (*Le Petit Café,* with his wife Yvonne Vallée); and the box-office bonanza directed by Ernst Lubitsch, *The Smiling Lieutenant* with Claudette Colbert and Miriam Hopkins (*Le Lieutenant Souriant,* with Colbert and Hopkins). Jesse Lasky, Adolph Zukor and production chief B. P. Schulberg were now hopeful that Jeanette and Chevalier could duplicate the lilting *The Love Parade.*

To appreciate the flavor that did come across in the new venture, *One Hour with You,* one must recall the behind-the-scenes situation at Paramount. Of all the major lots in Hollywood, that company was the most Continental, especially in the romantic inclinations of its star stable. Although top executive B. P. Schulberg was wed, it was an open secret that his chief love was contractee Sylvia Sidney, for whom he would venture anything, even putting his career on the line on several occasions. German import Marlene Dietrich had a spouse back in Germany, yet her constant companion in Hollywood was mentor/director Josef von Sternberg, and many voiced the thought that her penchant for wearing pants was a strange habit for a supposedly feminine woman. Claudette Colbert was stated to be wed to actor (later director) Norman Foster, but it was hardly the usual type of marriage. Young, talented Phillips Holmes suffered a nervous breakdown in the early Thirties and some reported that it stemmed from embarrassing sexual problems as well as tremendous career pressures. The much-married socialite Peggy Hopkins Joyce appeared on the lot for a film or two, and then there was Mae West. The Broadway phenomenon arrived in Hollywood in mid-1932 to join the Paramount forces. As she phrased it, "I'm not a little girl from a little town makin' good in a big town. I'm a big girl from a big town makin' good in a little town." After her debut in *Night After Night,* neither the movie industry nor Hollywood were ever the same.

By the time of making *One Hour with You,* even the less obser-vant members of the movie colony knew that boulevardier Chevalier and his talented wife Yvonne were undergoing domestic woes. At first his understanding dinner companion would be Miss Dietrich, but later sultry, dark-haired Kay Francis would become the prime target of Maurice's romancing. Strange that he should gravitate toward these two women, especially Miss Francis, who was reputed to have had quite a way with girls and liquor.

And Jeanette was not exactly a babe in the woods. The Hollywood grapevine was amazed by her relationship with Ritchie, a constant companion to her day and night. In the early Thirties, more than one journeyman of the Hollywood scene suspected Jeanette and Bob were secretly married. In fact, Walter Winchell started a feud (a *very rare* occurrence in Jeanette's life) with Miss MacDonald when he unchival-rously asserted that they were man and wife. Jeanette countered by offering, depending on who is to be believed, from $1,000 to $5,000 to the person who could prove she and Ritchie took wedding vows. Apparently there were no takers. The gossip would go to such lengths that Jeanette eventually issued a statement flatly denying the allega-tions.

I am not married to Bob Ritchie! I can't understand why people are so skeptical of the truth. Why should I deny it if we were married? Bob has been my closest friend and honest adviser. But the way I feel about my career and the time and effort I must devote to it, makes marriage out of the question for me until I am ready to retire.

Chevalier, himself, had his own views on the matter. In 1964 he would comment:

At the time we worked together she was very much in love with Bob Ritchie. But he, of course, was not the man for her. Their marriage, or arrangement—although I'm sure they were married, otherwise it's difficult to understand why she allowed him to mistreat her so—never seemed to interest any of the columnists or cause any gossip. And yet Ritchie would often come on the set, insult her, throw a jealous tantrum and leave after he had reduced her to tears. A moment later, when it was time to film a scene, she was ready to work, all smiles. I was not surprised when I later heard her referred to as "The Iron Butterfly," although I was surprised to hear she found that amusing. I never thought she had much of a sense of humor. When we worked together she always objected to anyone telling a risqué story.

Adding to the romantic turmoil on the Paramount lot was the usual dash of political intrigue, not to mention the studio's pending bankruptcy in the face of the growing Depression. Originally Lubitsch had been scheduled to direct *One Hour with You,* to insure his profitable magic as before. But he became intrigued with the project *The Man I Killed* (formerly called *Broken Lullaby*) and devoted his prime attention to that "serious" antiwar film. It was a film he felt he had to make and it was, for him, a one-of-a-kind effort. Nothing he was to do in the future would resemble this sad tale.

With Lubitsch engaged on a more dramatic front, George Cukor was asked to direct the property, a new version of a silent Lubitsch classic, *The Marriage Circle.* Cukor relates the narrative of events in an intelligent, informative fashion.

With the best intentions in the world, I couldn't do a Lubitsch picture. Lubitsch was what they really wanted and what they should have had.

I directed for about two weeks. I didn't like Chevalier, and he didn't like me, but Jeanette MacDonald and I subsequently became very good friends, and she wanted me to do a picture with her. We shot an English and French version simultaneously. Then B. P. Schulberg, head of the studio, saw a lot of rushes and didn't like them. Lubitsch had now

59

finished shooting *The Man I Killed,* but they didn't officially "remove" me. What happened was goddam agony for me. I was under contract and had to stay on the picture, on the set, while Lubitsch took over. . . .

Lubitsch still couldn't give a hundred percent of his time to it, because he was cutting the other picture and so on. I still did a few things, I carried them out the way he wanted, but for most of the time I just sat there and really did less than when I was a dialogue director.

I behaved very well, I think. I was very disciplined and acted as if I didn't mind. Officially I finished the picture, but Lubitsch really directed it.

Lubitsch did not reshoot Cukor's scenes, but left them intact.

I admire Lubitsch very much, but he shot things in a highly stylized way that is simply not my own. And we had a different approach to language. Lubitsch never really spoke English very well, and it didn't finally matter in his case, but it led him to do things I couldn't do. . . .

Anyway, after I'd sat on the set and watched Lubitsch direct, and minded my p's and q's, Mr. Schulberg called me into his office. "I'm going to ask you to do me a little favor," he said. Mind you, he was all-powerful, and I was less than the dust beneath his chariot wheels. "I'd like you to take your name off the picture," he said. And I refused. If he didn't want my name on the picture, he should have taken me off after the first two weeks. "Well," Mr. Schulberg said, "I'm taking your name off, anyway." I told him I'd sue, and I did. I wanted to leave the studio anyway.

The choice of an updated *Marriage Circle* script, with music by Oscar Straus, for Jeanette's first production either during or after the scandal, was timely. Here Jeanette plays Maurice's extremely jealous Parisian wife, who is at first ignorant of the unwanted advances of her friend (Genevieve Tobin) toward her husband. But Jeanette has been naughty too! She flirts with another (Charlie Ruggles), proving that two can play at the same game. In the course of the charming confection, Jeanette sings "It Was Only a Dream Kiss," duets "We Will Always Be Sweethearts" with Chevalier, and joins with her co-stars in a rendition of the title tune. Since this was still officially a Maurice Chevalier picture (his name was billed over the title), it was the Frenchman who had the bulk of songs to deliver: "What Would You Do?" "Oh, That Mitzi!" "What a Little Thing Like a Wedding Ring Can Do," and "Three Times a Day." Chevalier and Jeanette, under Lubitsch's direction, also made a French-language version of the film, entitled *Une Heure Pres De Toi.*

Both editions of *One Hour with You* were well-received, but once more Jeanette was overshadowed by Chevalier and the Lubitsch "touch." Mordaunt Hall of the *New York Times* found her "charming" and "graceful" and "in her element" in this smart operetta swirling in a contemporary French setting. The film itself was nominated for Best Picture of the Year but lost the Oscar to M-G-M's *Grand Hotel.*

Jeanette made many recordings in 1932, but several were rejected by Victor and had to be re-recorded. In Hollywood on April 24, accompanied by Nat W. Finston and the Paramount Studio Orchestra, she sang "One Hour with You" and "We Will Always Be Sweethearts," both of which were rejected, and the same songs in French, which were of acceptable quality. On April 27 she recorded the songs successfully, and re-recorded the title tune in French.

How ironic that in 1932 the queen and king of the Hollywood musical film, Jeanette and Maurice, were professionally attuned, but could not develop a rapport off camera. It must have caused the soprano many anxieties and only kindled the discontent that was saturating her relationship with Bob Ritchie. How strange Jeanette must have felt occupying a dressing room on the Paramount lot, with Maurice on one side, and his good friend Marlene Dietrich on the other.

For her next and what proved to be her final Paramount film, Jeanette was cast in *Love Me Tonight,* which may be safely regarded as one of the classic screen musicals of the Thirties.

Oddly enough, the man who directed the superior film, Rouben Mamoulian, did *not* want to make it. The odyssey follows.

One day shortly after I finished *Dr. Jekyll and Mr. Hyde* [with Fredric March and Miriam Hopkins], and everybody was happy about its prospects, I encountered Adolph Zukor on the lot. As you know, the executives of this era were often far more persuasive actors than the players under contract to them. Zukor, with tears in his eyes, implored me to produce and direct a film with Maurice Chevalier and Jeanette Mac-Donald. Both of them were under big salaried contracts to Paramount and, according to Zukor, the studio was on the brink of bankruptcy so it was imperative that stars like Chevalier and MacDonald be constantly used. I protested that I wasn't the man for the job, that Lubitsch had done very well with these two players in the past, and suggested Mr. Zukor approach him. But Lubitsch was busy with other projects, Zukor said, and wouldn't I please give it a try.

I promised to think about it, and the more I thought about it, the more interesting doing a light musical film became to me. But I couldn't find a suitable property. And then at a party, while talking to Leopold Marchand, a European writer then working at Paramount, I learned that he had a slight story idea that might be attractive. It was only two pages long, but when I read it, I thought it had a kind of fairy tale romantic magic, and I asked the studio to buy it.

I then got Richard Rodgers and Lorenz Hart to develop songs for the film. You understand, all the songs were carefully planned, with the lyrics to advance the story line, and their place in the story itself designed before the writers of the screenplay were engaged.

This is the way an original musical film should be developed, in my opinion, but it so seldom happens like this. When the screenwriters . . . came on the picture it was their job to construct the scenes and bridge the dialogue between the song numbers, so that the songs flowed from the action sequences and the actors didn't stop to sing a song. It worked perfectly.

Only Chevalier was, in the beginning, disturbed. He approached me one day and said, "I understand you're having story conferences on my next picture." I told him, yes, that was true, but I was first working with the song writers. He wondered why he wasn't included in the discussions.

Lubitsch, he said, always had him present at all preproduction meetings. I said that was all very well; that was the way Lubitsch worked; but Lubitsch wasn't doing *Love Me Tonight*—I was, and I worked my way, and I especially didn't want him on hand at my story conference. He was hurt and said he would complain to the front office. I told him to please do so, that I didn't want to do this picture and was only doing it as a great personal favor to Mr. Zukor, and would consider it a very special favor if he could get me taken off of it.

Maurice, of course, didn't go to the front office. He loved the script when it was shown to him, and was enchanted by all the Rodgers and Hart songs. *Love Me Tonight* turned out to be one of my happiest film productions, and I was delighted that it met with such critical and public favor when it was released.

On the whole, Mamoulian, as much a perfectionist and stylist as Lubitsch, had a cordial relationship with Jeanette on the set. But there were two items about which he occasionally criticized his leading lady: her infrequent but problematical bad taste in screen clothes, and more importantly, her penchant for allowing Bob Ritchie on the set.

Mamoulian felt it in the best interests of the production to bar Ritchie from the sound stages. That removed one obstacle. But one day Miss MacDonald came on the set wearing an atrocious dress. Her director ordered her to remove it and to find something more suitable from costumer Travis Banton's racks. She went off in a huff, but minutes later was back with another garment, not happy with letting her original choice go, but realizing who was boss. It seems here Mamoulian rarely had to use the lucky whistle he wore to discipline his errant stars.

The artfully concocted plot line has Chevalier as Maurice Courtelin, "the best tailor in France," who chases a money-owing titled customer (Charles Ruggles) to his country château. Along the way Maurice meets the attractive but icy Princess Jeanette (Jeanette), with whom he falls in love. At the château Maurice is introduced as a baron, and only after he has charmed everyone in sight is his ruse discovered. On the train back to Paris, he is heartbroken. But the repentant

Princess, concluding her strong love for the tailor is real, chases the train on horseback. In a marvelous moment, so typical of the Jeanette MacDonald persona, the Princess stands on the tracks, arms on hips, defying the train to pass over her. The train stops, of course, and the lovers are reunited. The finale occurs at the château in a vocal scene of conviviality. In the course of the ninety-minute musical, Jeanette has the opportunity to sing "Lover" and to duet with Chevalier "Love Me Tonight" and "Isn't It Romantic?"

Love Me Tonight, which premiered in August, 1932, was an immediate hit. While it did not single-handedly stem the tide of Paramount's debits, it earned a tidy profit. Jeanette was declared to be "as charming as ever" and her performance consolidated her star status in Hollywood. Credit was liberally sprinkled on Chevalier, Mamoulian, the composers and scripters, and the supporting cast, which included a tart Myrna Loy as the man-hungry Countess Valentine.

Before *Love Me Tonight* debuted, Jeanette was back at the Victor recording studios, making more records of the songs sung in the film. In Hollywood on July 5, accompanied by Nat Finston and the Paramount Studio Orchestra, she recorded English and French versions of the title songs, and English and French variations of "Isn't It Romantic?"

Love Me Tonight was to be Jeanette MacDonald's final film at Paramount. For some time, the studio had sought to cast her in non-singing roles, but she rebelled, probably remembering the apathetic reception of her Fox features, two of which had been straight comedies. Consequently, Paramount dropped her contract option, much in the way they let her go in 1930.

With the corporate accountants constantly warning of pending bankruptcy, Paramount could not afford to maintain a stable of high-priced, nonversatile players. The changing studio regime decided to gamble on the continuing success of iconoclastic Mae West, tough George Raft, handsome Gary Cooper and Cary Grant, exotic Marlene Dietrich, high-dramatic Sylvia Sidney and Miriam Hopkins, and decorative Claudette Colbert and Carole Lombard. In an economy wave they had already allowed Warner Bros. to "steal away" three of their highest-priced players: Ruth Chatterton, William Powell and Kay Francis. As for Chevalier, he would make two more pictures at Paramount before terminating his tenure there.

Jeanette paid for her individuality before reaping the huge rewards that followed. A new Jeanette MacDonald film did not appear until February, 1934, and her co-star was a fading silent screen idol. It was to be hoped she would not drift into cinematic oblivion with him.

CHAPTER FIVE

Fortunately, Europe had not forgotten Jeanette. Responding to generous offers from abroad, she set sail for the Continent in December, 1932. This time she was traveling as a respected performer rather than as a declaration that she was still alive. The concert-packed tour led her through Holland, Spain, Switzerland, Belgium and, of course, France. She made the healthy salary of $13,000 weekly through most of the trek, a fee that undoubtedly helped pay for a newly acquired villa in the picturesque south of France.

Just before the demanding tour began, Jeanette spent the holidays in the Antibes, often socializing with Basil and Ouida Rathbone (who would become good friends to the Raymonds), and Irving Thalberg and his actress wife, Norma Shearer. On Christmas night, they all went to the Sporting Club at Monte Carlo. Here another one of Jeanette's minor illusions was cracked.

> In the movies, we had pictured it so gaily, but that is not the real spirit of the place. Everyone is so tense, grim-faced, silent and determined to win. The players all look as though they are saying: "If I don't win on this turn of the wheel, I'll shoot myself!" It was not a very cheerful note for my Christmas—in fact, it made me so blue that I turned down all the parties for New Year's Eve and went to bed at ten o'clock."

Idealistic Jeanette might have been upset at the crassly professional attitude the amateur gamblers wore like a shield, but the woman Louella Parsons would later call the "greatest showman in Hollywood" did not forget her craft either. Despite being an envied movie star, a highly paid singer and the object of the affections of Bob Ritchie, she still had a lot of the little girl who schemed for attention in her. One night, the effervescent Basil Rathbones threw a typically plush party. It was agreed the men should come in black and the women in white. Norma Shearer arrived in blazing red and Jeanette made her entrance wearing lavender. One can only wonder who won the battle for attraction that evening.

While the vacation was not over for anyone, busy Irving Thalberg (still recuperating from his latest bout of overwork at Metro-Goldwyn-Mayer) was already making plans to star Jeanette in a series of M-G-M musicals. He was convinced that 1933 was the year of a renewed cycle of song-and-dance films. Word had already filtered to him of Warner Bros.' lavish *42nd Street*, which would reveal the expansive production genius of Busby Berkeley. And was not Metro itself planning to reunite its love team of Joan Crawford and Clark Gable in a glossy musical (to be called *Dancing Lady*)?

Actually Thalberg was in the process of setting up his own independent production unit at Metro—a compromise in his wager for power with mentor-rival Louis B. Mayer—and hoped to sign Jeanette to a personal contract. But Mayer seemed to have agents everywhere and he was well aware of the proximity of Thalberg and Miss MacDonald in Europe. Long before he had tried to woo Jeanette away from Paramount, but failed in his bid. Now he made the singing star such an attractive offer that she could not and would not refuse.

Jeanette was signed by M-G-M early in 1933, but did not return to Hollywood until her tremendously successful concert tour was completed. During the course of her European travels, many offers poured in from Milan, Rome, Berlin and the Opera Comique in Paris for the stage and screen star to sing opera. The opportunities were tempting, but perfectionist Jeanette knew she required far more operatic training and conditioning if she were to meet the rigid standards demanded by the world of high opera. She would wait until she was better prepared. After all, it was to be her final test as a performer. As she would explain it, "It is not that I prefer opera to concert, but somehow it seems that opera will be my final proof to myself. It will prove my original point: that I am a singer."

If some parties are to be believed, it was at this juncture that Jeanette took dramatic steps to begin severing her relationship from Bob Ritchie. *If* she had indeed been legally wed to him, it was at this time that she initiated clandestine divorce proceedings. *If* these legal manipulations did occur, they were so carefully disguised that some four decades later they still have not come to light.

On another level, there can be no doubt that part of the complex contractual arrangement between Jeanette and M-G-M required that for the first time in her film career, she place herself much more in the control of her employers. Not that she was to sacrifice certain prerogatives due any star of a major magnitude. But Louis B. Mayer and his executives made it quite clear to Jeanette that if a long-term investment were to be made in her screen career, she must be pliable to an overall pattern. In essence the scheme of things must emanate from Louis B. Mayer and not from the combined whims of Jeanette and her manager, Ritchie.

As Jeanette returned to Hollywood to enter a new phase of her career, she found that Hollywood itself had changed. To her mind, it was to the better.

Thanks to the screen antics of Miss Mae West and assorted other conspirators against "public decency," the motion picture industry had established a new, severer production code, under the tutelege of former postmaster general Will Hays. As cinema historian Miles Kreuger refers to Hays, this "self-inflicted arbiter of morality" caused some changes in the emphasis of certain genre films, and brought new life to that old stand-by, the costume spectacle.

Social comedies along the lines of those from Columbia Pictures' star director Frank Capra took the place of the tawdry, vivid sex comedies represented by Miss West and Jean Harlow. The brutal gangster film would go into a decline and former cinema tough guys like James Cagney and Edward G. Robinson would re-emerge—for a spell—as minions of the law, allowing for gory gun-downs of the bad guys. It seemed in the mid-Thirties that a screen rogue could be a rogue only if he were masked with a cloak of righteousness, as in the early movie characters of Errol Flynn. Thus violent gangster films were replaced by almost as violent, but more remote, costumed epics like *Captain Blood* and *Charge of the Light Brigade.*

How did all this affect the career of Jeanette MacDonald? It caused her to lose a savory part in a projected musical called *I Married an Angel.* The scenario was written especially for her, but the tale of an angel (Jeanette) who sacrifices her wings to marry a mortal could not pass through the heavenly gates of production guarded by Will Hays. Its authors, Rodgers and Hart, disgusted by this turn of events, re-shuffled the plotline to suit the stage, and turned it into a stage hit with Vera Zorina. Years later, the property would come back to haunt Jeanette.

While Metro was in a quandary as to how best to showcase their singing prima donna, Jeanette turned to Ritchie, who was still waiting patiently by. The duo signed a one-picture contract with United Artists to produce a property called *The Dutchess of Delmonico's.* Richard Wallace was to direct and Jeanette was to co-star with debonair Brit-isher Herbert Marshall. For some reason, the project never came to fruition.

In the midst of all this Jeanette was in constant communication with Elsie in Philadelphia, who was slowly recovering from a serious ailment. Actually, when her sister had been hospitalized, Jeanette had rushed back to Pennsylvania to be at her side.

Next Louis B. Mayer offered her a choice of two scripts, *The Cat and the Fiddle* and *The Merry Widow,* both musicals. She was unen-thusiastic about both of them.

Eventually company pressure forced Jeanette to make a selection. She chose *The Cat and the Fiddle* as her first project. From the Kern-Harback operetta, with a screenplay by Bella and Sam Spewack, the story concerns two lovers in Paris, played by Jeanette and Ramon Novarro. (His biggest success had been in the lead of the silent *Ben-Hur.* After initial semipopularity in talkies, his career had been declin-ing.) The hero becomes a success and Jeanette thinks he has forgotten her. But Jeanette returns to save his show, and romantically they find one another again. To direct the vehicle, Metro chose William K.

Howard, the man who had guided Jeanette through *Don't Bet on Women* at Fox. It was not a choice of her making.

When *The Cat and the Fiddle* debuted at the Capitol Theatre on February 16, 1934, Jeanette's mother and sister Blossom were in the audience. Appearing on the stage was Ramon Novarro singing "Pagan Love Song," "Long Ago in Alcala" and other tunes associated with his career. It was a significant moment for Jeanette. At that time and in that place, the past, present and future rolled into one unity. It was back in late 1919 that "broomstick legs" MacDonald made her debut in the *Demi-Tasse Revue* in the very same Capitol Theatre. The release of *The Cat and the Fiddle* signified the rejuvenation of Jeanette's film career. And her presence at M-G-M would lead to Jeanette becoming one of the greatest and most loved musical stars of all time.

The Cat and the Fiddle, with a score including "A New Love Is Old," "I Watched the Love Parade," "One Moment Alone," and "The Night Was Made for Love," was generally well received. The *New York Daily News* judged that "a gay and tuneful picture has been fashioned from the musical comedy." Everyone thought well of the performances of the stars, Jeanette and Novarro, and the supporting cast, including Frank Morgan, Charles Butterworth, Jean Hersholt and Vivienne Segal.

Yet *The Cat and the Fiddle*, with its final scene in glowing color, was not the full-blown hit M-G-M had expected. (Fox had suffered the same fate that year with Gloria Swanson's comeback project, *Music in the Air*.) According to Miss Segal, one of the reasons for the partial misfire of *The Cat and the Fiddle* was Jeanette. Miss Segal recollects that Metro had hired Bella and Sam Spewack to lighten the tone of the musical, and that in the transference, Vivienne Segal's vamp role had been emasculated. "It was fouled up so you wouldn't believe," says Miss Segal, "orders of Miss MacDonald. That was the picture that ruined my career. They absolutely ruined me. No one would cast me after that." The actress remembers that on the initial day of shooting, Jeanette paraded onto the set and greeted her co-player with, "Hello, Viv, have you seen your part? It stinks!"

Whatever the flaws of *The Cat and the Fiddle*, Louis B. Mayer decided to go ahead with the planned sound remake of *The Merry Widow*, the project that had caused so much artistic and financial chaos on the lot in the Twenties when autocratic Erich von Stroheim was directing Mae Murray and John Gilbert. Mayer had maneuvered Ernst Lubitsch over to Culver City and it was agreed that he would direct a resplendent version of the musical.

And at this time Chevalier, who had grown unhappy at Paramount, succumbed to the pleas of Mayer and Thalberg to join the M-G-M star family. It was promised that he would have some fresh roles that would revitalize his screen career. Yet for the first go-round at the new studio he agreed to play it safe by starring in familiar material, with songs, clothes and character that fit like three old shoes.

At first, Chevalier tried to convince Thalberg and the Metro officials into starring Grace Moore with him. But the studio had suffered badly in 1930–1931 when the Metropolitan opera star made two dismal entries for them. Would he not consider Jeanette MacDonald? The Frenchman's reticence against being reunited with her stemmed from the fact that 1) he disapproved of her reputed hauteur, especially in view of her ticklish situation with Bob Ritchie; 2) it would mean that now she was to be co-starred, not just featured, with him in a picture. His pride was at stake.

Meanwhile, Mayer was urging Jeanette to agree to starring in *Naughty Marietta.* He confided that he planned to bring Broadway-concert singing star Allan Jones to Hollywood to be her co-star, that as soon as an arrangement could be made with the Shuberts, his contract employers, he would be on his way to Culver City. Jeanette was not convinced. She was uncertain if the changing public tastes would respond to a cycle of operettas as they had a few years before. After all, now the big screen song-and-dance teams were proletarian Dick Powell and Ruby Keeler and the increasingly popular and swank Fred Astaire and Ginger Rogers. Mayer insisted he knew what the audiences wanted. He stressed that what Jeanette needed to do was to dismount from the high pedestal of opera and really pour her heart out to the paying customers in the galleries. To demonstrate the intent, Mayer got down on his knees and passionately sang an old Jewish lament, "Eli, Eli," and Jeanette was convinced.

However, difficulties arose with the Shuberts, who refused to release Jones for the project, and *Naughty Marietta* was temporarily shelved. Besides, the immediate problem at hand was casting *The Merry Widow.*

Grace Moore, who had returned to Hollywood to lower-case Columbia Pictures, relates how she coveted the assignment.

> I wanted to do *The Merry Widow* at M-G-M. I had heard that Thalberg was going to do it with Maurice Chevalier, but as yet had no widow. I begged extra time for a decision from Harry Cohn [about a Columbia film] and dashed over to the Metro lot to see Thalberg. How I wanted to do that picture! I used every art of persuasion I knew to convince Thalberg that I was his "widow." He was so kind but firm. "We're probably going to sign another singer," he admitted. Finally Thalberg told me bluntly that Lubitsch didn't want me, didn't believe in me, was sold on another girl.
>
> "I'll do it for nothing," I cried. "The role was made for me—the music for my voice."

She waited for another response in vain. All Thalberg would offer her was another option. She rejected it. Grace Moore instead went on to star in Columbia's *One Night of Love,* the 1934 film widely regarded as the first in a new series of operetta films whose popularity was to extend throughout the Thirties.

On the Metro lot, there was speculation that Lily Pons or Vivienne Segal might get the coveted role of Sonia, Marshovia's richest widow. For a time it was rumored that the vehicle would be converted into a dramatic presentation and that Joan Crawford would star in the project. Eventually it was decided to cast Jeanette.

When *The Merry Widow* finally got underway in 1934, it was given a terrific send-off with its $1,600,000 budget, an astronomical figure at the time. It has been said much of the money went to the two stars.

The typical Lubitsch touch was certainly present in *The Merry Widow:* ethereal extravaganza edged with satire. But 1934 Hollywood differed greatly from the city in 1929 when everyone was at once flustered and wondrous about sound.

The Hays Code of movie morality was administered rather stiffly by one of its main exponents, Joseph Breen. And since *The Merry Widow*'s smiling officer, Maurice Chevalier, was a rogue in rogue's clothing, problems were expected. At this time, practical Jeanette remarked, "The censors really can't do much about Chevalier. After all, there's no rule against a man having a naughty twinkle in his eyes, or seeming to have naughty thoughts, is there? Well, then. . . ."

Nevertheless, there was one major moment in the feature Breen did not like and demanded that it be re-shot. It is the sequence in which Chevalier picks Jeanette up, carries her across the room, dumps her on a couch, and sits in a chair beside her. As Jeanette explained (with a twinkle in *her* eyes), "The ruling was, that one is not supposed to play a scene in a horizontal position."

Lubitsch was amused, frustrated, disgusted, and bullied by this ruling, and begged Breen not to classify his harmless bit with other "horizontal" scenes. Finally, Breen decided to compromise. "He would let the scene go," Jeanette reported, *"providing* I kept my feet on the floor."

Although the feet are not visible throughout the entire scene, a brief shot shows her size 3½ C's clearly implanted on the floor. Very possibly *The Merry Widow* contains the wryest example of how screen love teams actually made love. The feet-on-the-floor ruling was to be a staple of soundstage romancing for years to come.

Not so oddly, the amours shared by Chevalier and Jeanette on screen were decidedly not repeated in real life. Jeanette was well aware that Maurice had wanted Grace Moore for his leading lady, and that he regarded Jeanette as a symbol of duplicity. Then too, during the early days of their initial film-making, Chevalier had made his traditional pass at his leading lady, and Jeanette had not forgotten this in the intervening years. She once called Chevalier "the fastest derriere pincher in Hollywood."

She also was upset because Chevalier, among others, touted her as being too conservative. It led to Jeanette defending her stance:

> I know I'm no prude. I'm not just guessing or hoping. I looked it up in the dictionary. It says: "Prude: a woman who makes an affected display of modesty or propriety." But my sharpest critics never hinted at any "affected display."
>
> So by dictionary standards, anyway, I'm cleared. Of course they used the word "priss" more often than "prude," and my dictionary doesn't give "priss." However, I won't

quarrel over terms. I'll admit the charges. I don't smoke or drink. I don't like risqué stories.

Some of the above statements should be qualified. First of all, she didn't smoke or drink because it would have been bad for her voice. Jeanette enjoyed a good joke as much as anyone—in fact, more—but the factor here was the teller. She never approved of overfamiliarity by mere acquaintances. If one was a friend, the situation was far different. One of Jeanette's primary personal statements was, "I've always made a point of controlling myself, because I always thought it was the thing to do." She could have wonderful, fun relationships with directors, such as W. S. Van Dyke II and Robert Z. Leonard, and could play practical jokes on them with flair, but business was business. She once remarked, "I've been told I have an Irish temper. I know I have Scottish thrift, and like the English I love a good show."

The Merry Widow was given a lavish premiere at the New York Astor Theatre on October 11, 1934. The event had all "the tumult and the shouting which befit . . . perhaps the coronation of emperors." Major Bowles, of radio fame, was the master of ceremonies for the gala, and he told the crowd gathered outside that there were enough stars present at the occasion to "outfit a new universe." Mounted police were required to keep the gathering orderly as the celebrities disembarked from the parade of limousines and proceeded into the theater. A breathless Jeanette MacDonald paused in the lobby to talk with Major Bowles and confessed that her "heart was filled with gratitude."

Neither the critics nor audiences were quite sure what to expect from the "new" *Merry Widow*. Those who had remembered the overt splendor and decadence of the von Stroheim silent epic might have anticipated a carry-over into the remake. Others hoped that the re-teaming of Chevalier-MacDonald-Lubitsch would bring to the fore the saucy spirit that had endeared their past screen efforts to the public—highbrows and lowbrows alike. After all, the premise of *The Merry Widow* had built-in spice and élan: when the gorgeous widow Sonia leaves Marshovia for Paris, the king is fearful that her departure will mean financial disaster (she controls over fifty percent of the country's resources, and the economy relies on her presence and expenditures). The ruler orders the devil-may-care Prince Danilo to Paris to woo the widow and entice her back to Marshovia. They meet in the French capital but each is unaware of the other's true identity. Later in Marshovia she learns the truth, and although hurt by the betrayal testifies in his behalf at his court-martial. Despite all, he is convicted and jailed. She visits him in his cell and the king has her locked in with Danilo until she consents to wed him.

If contemporary critics are to be relied upon, *The Merry Widow* fulfilled everyone's artistic and entertainment goals. "It is a good show in the excellent Lubitsch manner, heady as the foam on champagne, fragile as mist and as delicately gay as the good-natured censor will permit" *(New York Times)*. "There is charm and effervescence . . . permeating, and entertainment. One possibly should not ask for more" *(Los Angeles Times)*. "The former Paramount pair once again work beautifully in harness, with this one a cinch to enhance Miss MacDonald's already high rating as a singer and looker, and a good bet to regain much of the ground lost by Chevalier in the last couple of years" *(Weekly Variety)*.

For most, there was an excellent balance between the rakish Danilo who sings "Girls, Girls, Girls," "Widows Are Gay," and "I'm Going to Maxime's" and the haughty but adventuresome Sonia who vocalizes "Villa" and "Tonight Will Teach Me to Forget." Together they sing and dance to the hauntingly grandiose "The Merry Widow Waltz."

No expense was spared to make the production as technically sumptuous as possible. Adrian created the gowns, with Ali Hubert designing the men's costumes. Lorenz Hart and Gus Kahn joined with Richard Rodgers to contribute the new music; Cedric Gibbons and Fredric Hope provided the plush art decor (for which they won Oscars) and Oliver T. Marsh was the ace cinematographer who photographed Chevalier to look younger and Jeanette to look even more luscious than in her Paramount days. And few could complain of the witty, well-paced scenario by Ernest Vajda and Samson Raphaelson, which brought new life to the familiar plot line of the original operetta.

So enthused was Metro by *The Merry Widow* that they had implored the principals to perform in a French version of the film, entitled *La Veuve Joyeuse,* with Akim Tamiroff, Fifi D'Orsay, Georges Renavent, Lya Lys, et al supporting them.

Yet *The Merry Widow* was not a money-maker; the original investment had been too costly. Chevalier and the studio would soon come to a parting of the ways. It had originally been agreed upon that Chevalier would thereafter star in versions of *The Chocolate Soldier,* a romantic comedy called *Escapade,* and a musicalized rendition of *The Last of Mrs. Cheyney.* Thalberg even agreed to team Grace Moore with Maurice in *The Chocolate Soldier.* However, when it was learned that Miss Moore was to be given co-starring billing, the French singer politely declined. He felt it would be a step backward in his career. Instead, he negotiated a cancellation of his M-G-M contract. It would be twenty-four years before Chevalier would star in another Metro film, making a triumphant American comeback in *Gigi* in 1958.

As for Jeanette, Louis B. Mayer was not about to give up on the box-office potential of this woman whom he had idolized for years. Just as in the Forties he would succumb to the ladylike charms of Britisher Greer Garson, so now he coveted—in all senses of the word—Miss MacDonald.

For Mayer, Jeanette presented a schizoid situation. If Jeanette had ever submitted to Mayer's many advances (as with Myrna Loy, he had propositioned her on several occasions), he would have been disillusioned forever about her enviable status as a woman of high respectability. The fact that he could not woo her sexually no doubt pushed him harder to enhance her reputation as a figure on and off the screen, as a mythical woman of the highest qualities. It made his courtship failure more acceptable to him.

Thus, despite the unpromising public response to *The Merry Widow,* Mayer had Jeanette's contract renegotiated. She would be part of the M-G-M family for five years and in that time, most anything could happen. Perhaps his wildest sexual dreams would come true.

Meanwhile, late in 1934, Jeanette returned to the recording studio, and disked several of the songs from her two Metro features. On August 14, she recorded, from *The Merry Widow,* "I Love You So," in both English and French, along with "Villa" in two languages. Both French versions were rejected by Victor. On August 30 she recorded English and Gallic versions of "Tonight Will Teach Me to Forget" from *The Cat and the Fiddle,* and the French was rejected. Back again on September 20, Jeanette sang "Try to Forget" from *The Cat and the Fiddle,* and the French rendition was shelved.

Naughty Marietta and superstardom lay just around the bend in 1935 for Jeanette. It was well-known on the lot that she did not like the script, but was persuaded by Mayer that schmaltz was the public's current desire. She was assigned to the role of Princess Maria in this low-budget "A" film.

But the casting of Captain Warrington, the male lead, was another situation entirely. Mayer had wanted to film the project for several years, but a suitable Warrington could not be found. The studio had suffered in its attempt to make Metropolitan Opera star Lawrence Tibbett into a marketable commodity, and no one else had come immediately to mind. That is, until Mayer was alerted to the potentials of handsome, Welsh-descended Allan Jones, whose highly regarded tenor voice had won him the respect of concert and Broadway audiences alike. As mentioned before, Mayer and M-G-M instituted negotiations with the Shubert Brothers to acquire Jones' screen services. All seemed ready for the start of filming and *Naughty Marietta* was put into pre-production.

As Allan Jones told this author recently, "Then the Shuberts put a stipulation to the agreement that I would have to pay $50,000 to buy my way out of the contract." Since M-G-M was fearful of becoming embroiled in a complex lawsuit (threatened by the Shuberts), it was up to Jones to find the large sum on his own. He flew to St. Louis to speak to a benefactor from his Municipal Opera days. Jones recalls, "He told me, 'Allan, you didn't have to come all this way to ask me. The money is yours. It is in your bank account now.' I was so excited I flew directly back to New York without thinking to contact Metro." As it turned out the studio had been desperately trying to find Jones all that day. They could delay no longer; they had to cast the part. "So I lost the role and Jeanette MacDonald and Nelson Eddy became the new love team."

Nelson Eddy had been contracted to Metro since 1933, and had appeared in three films, with a specialty number in each. The handsome and popular young baritone did not really want a film career, but thought the publicity would boost his already impressive concert standing.

The story of his arrival in Los Angeles is worth repeating. A prominent artist scheduled to perform at the Los Angeles Philharmonic had to cancel suddenly due to illness. A wire was sent to New York, begging for a speedy replacement. Nelson Eddy, then making his western debut in San Diego, was recommended. Los Angeles wired back to New York that Eddy was an unknown quantity to them. Assured of the young man's talents, he was contacted, and switched bookings in order to make the substitution. In the audience the night of Eddy's Los Angeles appearance was a talent scout from RKO. He persuaded Nelson to make a screen test at his studio. Ultimately, the blond singer was also auditioned at M-G-M and Paramount.

Mark Sandrich, director of some of the Fred Astaire–Ginger Rogers musicals, recommended that RKO place Nelson under contract. That company was suffering financial reverses and was asking its roster of players to take salary cuts, so the best they could offer was approximately half of what Eddy had expected. He refused. Disgusted with the ways of Hollywood, he packed his bags and went east to return to the concert stage.

But Ida Koverman, executive assistant of Louis B. Mayer and a musician herself, convinced the boss to bring Eddy back to Hollywood. She reasoned the baritone's popularity made it worth the trouble to take another look. In 1933 Eddy was contracted to Metro. Unfortunately, the musical operetta had yet to make a comeback, and Nelson idled. His seven-year contract must have seemed a dreadful error of judgment, preventing the singer from doing what he really wanted to do—sing.

Nelson appeared in three M-G-M films, *Broadway to Hollywood* and *Dancing Lady* in 1933, and *Student Tour* in 1934. How he got the first of his miniscule roles is intriguing. According to director George Sidney, "A singer named Gene Mallin was coming out of a café when he accidentally put his car in reverse and went off the pier. He had a small role in a film and rather than wait for him to recover from his injuries, word went out to find somebody who fit his wardrobe. A nobody named Nelson Eddy was just large enough, and they threw him into Gene's clothes." None of the parts in his Metro films satisfied Eddy or justified his huge salary.

At one time, the studio thought of casting Eddy with another newly signed singer, Jeanette MacDonald, in a musical version of *The Prisoner of Zenda,* but that idea collapsed.

Mayer called a meeting of his executive staff, and after some deliberation, announced he wanted to film *Naughty Marietta* with Nelson Eddy substituting for Allan Jones. Some sources have suggested that it was Jeanette who picked Nelson as her co-star from a batch of photos.

By the time *Naughty Marietta* began shooting with the principals, Jeanette and Eddy were well acquainted. According to the publicity mill they even dated and it was she who had convinced him to remain in Hollywood, while he in turn inspired her to think about singing grand opera. It all sounded nice and the gullible public was ready to believe it.

It was also about this time that Bob Ritchie exited from Jeanette's life. Before 1935 was through she had transferred her business affairs to other capable hands, and thereafter usually relied on public relations expert and friend Helen Ferguson for professional advice. As the years passed, Ritchie would gravitate into film and television distribution. On June 15, 1972, then an obscure figure from the past, he died of cancer in Manhattan, survived by a brother and sister. In his modest apartment at 108 East 38th Street several dozen safety deposit keys were found, leading to the speculation that perhaps, like W. C. Fields, he had stashed money away in a series of banks across the country.

Back on the *Naughty Marietta* set, W. S. Van Dyke II was in charge—and for a very good reason. He was known as "One Take" Van Dyke in Hollywood and could whip through a script of any sort in the breeziest and most efficient manner. The previous year he had shot *The Thin Man* in twelve days, producing not only a million-dollar-earning murder mystery classic, but establishing the highly lucrative screen team of William Powell and Myrna Loy. Perhaps he could work the same wonders with Jeanette and Nelson and help recoup some of the expenses of *The Merry Widow.*

Van Dyke and Jeanette, from the start, saw eye to eye on the project and its filming. They both agreed that it was necessary to instill confidence into Eddy so that he would provide a relaxed performance on camera. The studio readily agreed to Eddy's request to bring his vocal coach Dr. Edouard Lippe onto the set. In fact, the learned teacher was given a bit in the picture in the inn scene.

80

On the first day of shooting, Van Dyke wanted to start with the bit of Lippe climbing the lamp post to light the wick. The director briefed the coach, sat down, and the whistle blew. "Quiet! Roll 'em!" echoed across the soundstage, but no one moved. Van Dyke said jokingly, "I've had 'em green, but never this green before!"

Nelson was then rehearsing his lines across the expansive stage, and he was called to shoot one of his sequences. "Do you know your lines, kid?" the director inquired. Nelson nervously replied in the affirmative, and the camera soon was rolling. Nelson opened his mouth to speak, but nothing came out. Van Dyke sympathized and told him to rehearse some more, and come back later.

Jeanette then popped out of her portable dressing room and complained about a hat producer Hunt Stromberg wanted her to wear. "You know it's not my type." "Well, it is kind of small," he chuckled. Before he could comment further, Jeanette pulled out a big blue hat trimmed with ostrich feathers. "Wardrobe designed this one," she said hopefully. "I want to wear this." She put on both hats, one at a time. Wearing the first with a grim face, she lit up upon topping her head with the larger one. Van Dyke knew when he was licked. "Fat chance I've got of telling you which one you're going to wear. Wear the big one!" Van Dyke was no Rouben Mamoulian here, but he was definitely the boss on the set, and he and Jeanette shared many happy moments together on the sound stages and as friends after hours.

In fact there was quite a give-and-take between director and leading actress. Van Dyke was fond of giving parties for the girls in the cast, get-togethers that would last far into the night. But he thought nothing of giving them early morning calls for the group scenes. As a jovial bit of revenge, Jeanette sponsored her own after-hours soiree, with Van Dyke the only man present. She served her specialty (baked beans with a thick sauce) and kept him dancing with the girls for four hours straight. He got the message.

Thanks to all the clowning around, Nelson was a bit freer in his performance. But he still had problems. One scene with Jeanette turned out to be unexpectedly funny. In the shot, Nelson takes her arm. But the overzealous neophyte actor paid more attention to her than to his pathway on the set. He walked into a tree. Nelson continued and Van Dyke was so amused he left the clumsy bit in the scene.

During the course of production of this black-and-white *Naughty*

Marietta Jeanette had to devote much time to preparation, as her Louis XV costumes and hairdos were rather extravagant. Often as not she could be found on the sound stage sidelines situated in her pink-satin-upholstered leaning board, leaning into relaxation at an oblique angle so as not to ruffle her wardrobe. But on this one particular occasion she had spent the better part of the day in her dressing room, waiting for her hair to dry. Her wardrobe mistress suggested she view the previous day's rushes in the projection room, so off she went. Van Dyke soon called for her, and was told by someone that his star was off watching a movie. He fumed. "Well, that's just dandy. I'm holding up an entire company while my leading lady is enjoying a movie." Deciding not to wait for Jeanette's beck and call, he dismissed the cast and crew, and everybody departed.

Later Jeanette returned to find a deserted set, lit only by the usual night lamp cast in the middle of the stage. Discovering that the director ended shooting without consulting her, she flew into fury and stormed in on production executive Eddie Mannix. Nothing could be determined about Van Dyke's whereabouts, and Mannix advised her to be on the set first thing in the morning, and explain herself to Van Dyke.

Disturbed by the whole affair, she decided to joke her way out of it. Calling Harry Albiez in the prop department, she arranged to be pulled out on the studio floor the next morning in a huge doghouse. At 8:55 A.M. six stagehands carried the structure onto the set, and placed it in front of Van Dyke. A tiny white arm popped out and gave the director an apple. As he was about to launch into the lecture he had prepared, Jeanette stuck her head out and pleaded, "And now may I come out, please, humm, Mr. Boss Man, may I please, Hummm?" Van Dyke was destroyed with laughter, and his tirade forgotten. From then on, the two had a great time playing jokes on each other on every production they worked on together.

But Nelson Eddy was still frightfully stiff in front of the camera. One day Van Dyke became so annoyed that he screamed in despair, "I've handled Indians, African natives, South Sea Islanders, rhinos, pygmies, and Eskimos and made them act—but not Nelson Eddy."

Although the remark was not intended for Eddy's ears, nor was it completely serious, the young baritone had had enough. But Woody smoothed matters over and came up with an idea which may have saved

Eddy's film career. He decided to let Nelson record his songs, not in front of cameras and lights, but in a recording studio, with an orchestra.

The singer still had problems, but one by one, they were eliminated. Eddy could not always hit the high notes, so Van Dyke informed him he would cut the music to the shot set-ups, and would therefore miss the unmouthed tones. At one point, Eddy made up his mind to finish the song. The orchestra swelled to a climax, and as Nelson was just about to hit the high note, an incredible shriek destroyed the take. It was Van Dyke's method of loosening up Nelson—and it worked. The two became fast friends.

Jeanette hoped that Van Dyke would not pull any such prank on her. She was wrong. One day when they were to synchronize Jeanette's recording of "The Italian Street Song," Van Dyke got his "revenge" for the doghouse trick. The sequence was to be shot silent, and Woody played the melody twice, to give Jeanette the proper feel of it. As the cameras started to roll, Jeanette opened her mouth only to discover a blast of Chinese music was blaring from the loudspeakers. She was nervous before the number, but then upon seeing Van Dyke laughing off to the side, she joined in the guffaws.

Everybody was at ease, and those Three Musketeers of Mirth and Music, MacDonald, Eddy, and Van Dyke, went on to complete one of the most successful film operettas in screen history. Before it was produced by M-G-M, *Naughty Marietta* by Rudolf Friml was considered one of the five greatest comic operettas composed, along with DeKoven's *Robin Hood* and Victor Herbert's *Serenade, Fortune Teller* and *Mlle. Modiste.* Gus Kahn was hired to adapt the lyrics of the 1910 operetta for the contemporary screen and Douglas Shearer's sound recording was so sparkling that he won an Oscar. *Photoplay* magazine would bestow its Movie of the Year Award on *Naughty Marietta.*

Perhaps the keenest element in creating the overwhelming public acceptance of *Naughty Marietta* was that it avoided pomposity at all costs. Jeanette may have provided exaggerated nuances as Princess Marie de la Bonfain, and Eddy's Captain Richard Warrington all too often resembled a stuffed mannequin. But the heroine and hero of this musical soap opera were such romanticized prototypes of most filmgoers' dreams of themselves that it all worked marvelously well. To the joy of audiences, Jeanette's character had a wonderful tongue-in-cheek quality, which counterbalanced any possibility of the vehicle being too airy and starchy. Each star had a share of solo songs: Jeanette with "The Italian Street Song," Nelson with the virile "Tramp Tramp Tramp" in accompaniment with the Louisiana woodsmen. And together the couple sang the enduring melody, "Ah, Sweet Mystery of Life."

Ed Sullivan in the *New York Daily News* bragged that "Mac-Donald-Eddy are the new team sensation of the industry." Eileen Creelman *(New York Sun)* raved, "Jeanette MacDonald is at the top!" *New York World Telegram*'s William Boehnel proclaimed, "Mac-Donald's is a stunning performance both vocally and dramatically." The film went on to become one of the year's big money-makers for the studio, along with *A Night at the Opera, Broadway Melody of 1936, Mutiny on the Bounty, China Seas,* and *A Tale of Two Cities.*

Understandably, Jeanette was now high on film musicals, and she gave forth with some concepts of their nature. "Musical drama of the screen must primarily be drama because, whether musical or not, a picture to be acceptable to a screen audience must be believed." But she qualified her remarks. "In musical comedy, the music is stressed rather than the plot and the audience can accept this."

The public was now more anxious than ever to know every little detail available about Jeanette. The fan magazines sought to fill this gap. It was revealed that she had moved into a lavish new house with her mother. It had a Louis XV living room with green walls and green drapes with gold brocaded satin and upholstered doors imported from an old French château. Her bedroom opened into a small patio. The clock and candelabra were composed of Dresden china, the bedroom mirror had a frame of twisted gold. A tapestry fire screen shielded the fireplace. Her dressing table boasted a glass top with flounces of delicate lace peach over pearl satin. The drapes were peach brocaded satin. Toilet articles were hammered silver, small lamps on her dressing tables had delicate metal bases, with pink parchment shades. The walls were light cream stucco, and the furniture was finished in light walnut.

According to the publicity releases of the day, Jeanette liked practical jokes, and had nicknames for all her co-workers. She enjoyed a crowd while singing in front of the camera, but preferred privacy for sad or emotional scenes. At night before retiring, she read mystery and thriller novels, and before she turned out the lights on the thousands of tiny articles, statuettes and fans she collected, she made sure her three dogs were bedded down.

During the early salad years, Jeanette kept faithfully to a diet, which did give her some leeway. For breakfast, she had fruit with warm milk. Lunch was often string beans, potatoes, and squash. Dinner varied. But when a film was in production, she had to eat as much as five times the normal amount, to compensate for lost energy. Anything consumed during the course of the shooting day was accomplished in her portable dressing room.

As a fast-rising movieland prima donna, Jeanette began giving advice to aspiring singers. She once said, "Always be natural, never let anyone talk you out of singing naturally."

After the success of *Naughty Marietta,* there was no question that Nelson Eddy was now a viable screen commodity. Ironically by this time Allan Jones had arrived on the Metro lot and willingly would have done any of the roles that were to go to Eddy over the subsequent years. Meanwhile with the success of Grace Moore at Columbia, Metro offered to star her in *Rose-Marie* with Eddy as her leading man. But she objected to the "unknown." Thus the project evolved as a Jeanette-Nelson Eddy vehicle, and for good measure Allan Jones was cast in a supporting role.

Originally this Rudolph Friml operetta had enjoyed a 557-performance run on Broadway in 1924, and then had been turned into an M-G-M silent feature in 1928 with Joan Crawford and James Murray. Metro hoped the new version would prove the publicity which announced the film as "Lovers' heartbeats set to enchanting music."

The story line of Friml's operetta was revamped to the needs of MacDonald-Eddy. The film itself showed that a musical could be taken out of doors—thanks to director W. S. Van Dyke II—and not lose any of its powers, and also benefit from a naturalistic note.

Of course, filming outside studio gates made nature a significant factor in the shooting schedule. Time after time, director Van Dyke had to wait for a cloud to pass by to get a necessary shot.

Reaching the location site was a problem in itself. Much of the film was shot in the Lake Tahoe area of northern California. A special train of seventeen box cars was necessary to ship the equipment to a location in the High Sierras. A series of totem poles forty feet high were built on a state-owned area at Emerald Bay for the Indian totem pole dance number staged by Chester Hale. A chuck wagon followed the cast and crew around the Sierras serving cold meals. Over seven hundred Indians and two to three hundred white people made this no easy task. They solved this problem by serving box lunches.

One day the prop department decided to provide Van Dyke with a treat. They set up a small table for him outside his tent, and served a nice salad and hot beef stew. Van Dyke sat down and asked skeptically, "Is this the same thing everybody else is getting for lunch?" When answered negatively, he rose and said, "I'm sorry, boys, I thought you knew there would be no discrimination in this unit." He proceeded to go to the end of the line for his box lunch.

Eddy had his share of location problems. On one occasion the script called for him to hop on a horse and ride off. Van Dyke, an expert horseman, showed him how. Nelson tried it, and overzealous as usual, jumped right over the horse into the bushes. The horse galloped off alone. More to his liking, he and Jeanette would entertain the locals every Sunday morning with renditions of "Indian Love Call" and other songs from *Rose-Marie.*

Jeanette was not always on the sidelines when production problems occurred. "One Take" Van Dyke was about to film a scene that required Jeanette to tumble off a horse and fall into the river. To obtain the necessary close shots, Jeanette was lowered into the studio water tank, from which she could not rise without help. In fact, only by lowering a ladder could anyone enter or leave the contraption. This was done to give the boom a clear field. Although the tank was not holding much water, enough was in it to make one feel uncomfortable. Van Dyke was shooting his close-ups and twelve A.M. was fast approaching. Jeanette wondered about this. After the last shot, the noon whistle blew, and everyone promptly vanished.

Jeanette sat there alone, in deadly silence. She realized she was the victim of yet another Woody Van Dyke special. Refusing to cry for help, she remained there alone for a few minutes. Soon, Van Dyke crept over, and peered down into the tank. "You little devil," he said with mild frustration, "I might have known you'd drown before you'd ever yell for help." With that, a ladder was quickly lowered and Jeanette was hauled out of the tank—wet and annoyed at her jokester director.

Perhaps the most audacious practical joke pulled during the elaborate production of *Rose-Marie* had Dr. Edouard Lippe as its special victim. Always asking questions, the short man noticed one day that every time Van Dyke yelled "Turn 'em," the cameraman flicked a switch on a box attached to the camera. Grabbing at the chance for a put-on, Van Dyke informed the vocal coach that the little switch actually shut down *all* activity on the lot while he was shooting.

One morning Lippe asked if he might have the honor of pulling the switch. Cameraman Bill Daniels agreed, and the prank went into operation. When Daniels signalled, Lippe turned the switch. Immediately a series of explosions occurred, and Daniels was "horrified" as his camera blew up and the film went flying in several directions. Lights crashed to the floor and scenery tumbled down (on cue). Men and women ran frantically about and Van Dyke shouted, "Who threw that switch?"

From behind a cloud of smoke, a chagrined Lippe offered, "Me." "Do you know what you've done?" cried Woody, pulling at his hair in mock anguish. When Lippe apologized and insisted he would pay for the damaged film, the set broke up, and the joke was revealed. (Electricians and prop men had worked the night before setting up the elaborate scheme, and "Pop" Arnold and crew members blasted shotguns out of sight to imitate explosions.)

Years later, Jeanette would say of the director, "I found Van Dyke so enigmatical and yet compatible, and then again absolutely pious at times—but always with the most delightful sense of humor!" Eddy would remember, "That man's honesty is a rare virtue. The thing that impressed me the most from the time I first met him was his absolute frankness."

But everything was not levity during the making of *Rose-Marie*. While Eddy was unmindful of the showy little role given lanky Jimmy Stewart as Jeanette's errant brother, he was constantly on guard about the presence of Allan Jones in the few opera-within-the-story sequences. In fact, after the staging of the operatic scenes from *Romeo and Juliet* (the waltz song "Je Veux Vivre dans Ce Reve" and the death scene) and *Tosca* ("He Asked Thy Life or My Love" from Act III of the Puccini opera), Eddy went to the Metro heads and announced that unless Jones' footage was trimmed, there would be great difficulty with Mr. Eddy in the future. Despite the fact that Hunt Stromberg was and would remain a staunch ally of Jones, he had no other option but to accede to Nelson's demands. Thus there is less of Allan Jones in the release print than intended.

For a girl who maintained only a "C" average at Julia Richmond High School in New York (while in the *Demi-Tasse Revue* and thereafter), Jeanette could not be faulted for her astuteness in judging what the audience expected of her. In *Naughty Marietta* she performed a bit of pantomime that never failed to amuse viewers or to gain their sympathy for her characterization. It was the moment when she embarks for America, in the disguise of her servant, who has become one of the casquette girls leaving for Louisiana to wed a colonist. To avoid detection from the soldiers searching for the Princess she screws up her face as she chomps on a crust of bread, allowing her spectacles to fall down on her nose. In *Rose-Marie* Jeanette furthers the gimmick. In her wilderness trek to find her brother, she finds herself without funds and forced to entertain at a frontier saloon to earn her keep. There (famed shimmy) dancer Gilda Gray advises the prima donna on the art of delivering a number for the barroom set. This evolves in Jeanette's Marie de Flor singing bits of "Dinah" and "Some of These Days" in a pseudo-pop style, showing movie audiences that she could, after all, be plain folk.

As *Naughty Marietta* had the entrancing "Ah, Sweet Mystery of Life," *Rose-Marie* was especially memorable for its duet, "Indian Love Call," sung in the rugged outdoors. It outdid *Naughty Marietta* in box-office receipts.

Not forgetting her recording career, Jeanette went into the studio on March 20, 1935 (before *Rose-Marie*), to record English and French versions of the "Italian Street Song" and two English variations of "Ah, Sweet Mystery of Life."

Jeanette always had a sharp eye for story line and many said would have made a superior film producer (an aspect she sought to try later in her career). Her next project was conceived several years before production. Robert Hopkins, a former silent screen title writer known around the studio as "Hoppy," had written a story about a man called Wilson Mizner. He brought the idea to Irving Thalberg. Thalberg was enthusiastic and told Hoppy and his friend Anita Loos to go ahead and fashion a script. They called it *San Francisco,* and named the Mizner character "Blackie Norton."

Before production could get underway, Thalberg became ill (he would die in September, 1936) and Louis B. Mayer assigned Bernard Hyman to the project. Anita Loos has described Hyman as "a victim of that special Hollywood naiveté that's incapable of recognizing bad taste, most of all his own." There were also problems with Hollywood's premier censor, Joseph Breen. There is a scene in *San Francisco,* where Blackie Norton, owner of a "sinful" Frisco nightclub on the Barbary Coast, knocks down his nemesis, a priest named Father Tim. They argue over a singer in Norton's employ called Mary. Breen felt the public would take the side of Norton (since Clark Gable was touted for the role) and not jeer him for the violent act toward the church and the Father's jaw.

A Father Benedict came up with a solution that basically pleased all concerned. The new scene took place in the gym. An expert boxer, Father Tim allows Blackie to knock him out on purpose, to show the man of God "turning the other cheek" and, thus, emerging as a hero.

But *San Francisco* almost did *not* feature Gable as Norton. Some time before production was to start, "Hoppy" took his script idea to Jeanette. She was impressed with the story. The theme concerned the regeneration of a saloon owner (Norton) through the hands of childhood friend Father Tim, singer Mary, and a little help from the 1906 Frisco earthquake.

The studio wanted Jeanette to be the big name in this epic, but she realized it was the story that counted, and pushed for Gable as her leading man. She even checked out Hopkins' background, to make sure he could handle the scripting, and then went into a fighting position, to push for the right cast and story.

But self-willed Gable did not want to make the film. He had just finished one epic, *Mutiny on the Bounty,* and that was enough for him. Since he knew Jeanette was to be a star, he assumed it was to be a musical. Gable did not want to be upstaged by a prima donna. Besides, he was going on a well-deserved vacation.

One day persistent Jeanette confronted Gable about the project. He told her in no uncertain terms, "Look here, Miss MacDonald, I want to go hunting"—and before he could finish, Jeanette begged him to read the script. He read the scenario and loved it, but he was still not convinced about co-starring with a "prima donna." He did not want to have sit around on camera twitching his ears while she belted out a song.

But Gable had not counted on Jeanette's persuasiveness. When he learned that she had given up a chance to make another film which would have earned her $170,000 (she was on a per film fee) in order to do *San Francisco* with Gable, he was impressed. When she promised that she would not sing in any scene shared with him, *unless* he so desired, he was more impressed. When she hounded the casting office to assign Spencer Tracy as Father Tim, he was convinced that Miss MacDonald was a pro worth working with then and there.

M-G-M's research department did a tremendous job of recreating 1906 San Francisco both before and after the earthquake. Studio bosses dictated that all destruction in the film had to be honest depictions of the property destroyed, or the company might be faced with ruinous libel suits. Since all records were lost in the quake, the task was doubly difficult. Some of the locations constructed for the epic were the Barbary Coast's Paradise Café, an old Grand Opera House, the Poodle Dog Restaurant, the Palace Hotel which then housed the New York Metropolitan Opera Company, Schutzer Park, Cliff House, Lyric Hill and the Grenable Hotel.

Even Gable had to study old-time slang, to fit into the turn-of-the-century picture of the topical anti-hero. Some of the expressions he learned were "take a gander," which means "get out of here"; "everybody stew," which translates "everybody dance"; "Horse the show," which tells one he has been "monopolizing the performance."

W. S. Van Dyke II, veteran of two Jeanette MacDonald films and several Gable-starring vehicles, was contracted to direct *San Francisco*. Anita Loos spoke of Woody, "But no sooner did he start filming than Hoppy and I realized we again faced disaster. Van Dyke, who was capable of understanding the mentality of South Sea savages, was an oaf when it came to the subtleties of the San Francisco tenderloin." On the other hand, Van Dyke was the kind of tough director Gable was partial to, and a proven talent as far as Jeanette was concerned.

In the lengthy course of production, there were some on-the-set miscalculations that pushed back the filming schedule a bit, but maintained the company's sanity under front office pressure to complete the expensive picture. During a rehearsal of the *La Traviata* scene, Jeanette's character takes a curtain call. The curtain was supposed to be pulled back for her graceful exit. Instead, it got caught in her skirts. A frantic heroine had to call for help. Generally able to find some humor in a situation, she said, "Maybe they can use this situation for the next Marx Brothers picture."

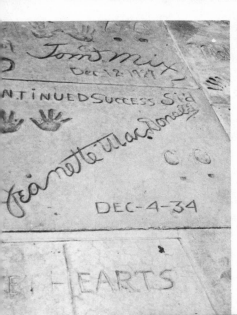

HER PRINTS AT
GRAUMAN'S
CHINESE THEATRE
(DECEMBER 4, '32).

WITH LOUIS B. MAYER
IN THE MID-THIRTIES.

ON THE SET OF *ROSE-MARIE* ('36)
WITH DIRECTOR WOODY
VAN DYKE II (RIGHT) AND
NELSON EDDY AND
JAMES STEWART IN BACK ROW.

WITH MAURICE CHEVALIER
IN *THE MERRY WIDOW* ('34).

ON THE SET OF
MAYTIME ('37)
WITH
JOHN BARRYMORE.

WITH NELSON EDDY IN *MAYTIM*

IN *THE FIREFLY*
WITH ALLAN JONES.

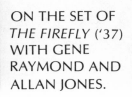

ON THE SET OF
THE FIREFLY ('37)
WITH GENE
RAYMOND AND
ALLAN JONES.

WITH GROOM GENE RAYMOND
AT THEIR WEDDING (JUNE 16, '37).

THE WEDDING PARTY INCLUDING:
NELSON EDDY, ALLAN JONES, BLOSSOM,
FAY WRAY, GINGER ROGERS, JOHNNY MACK
BROWN AND BASIL RATHBONE.

WITH LEO CARRILLO AND NELSON EDDY IN
THE GIRL OF THE GOLDEN WEST ('38).

WITH TERRY KILBURN
AND NELSON EDDY
IN *SWEETHEARTS* ('38).

WITH GRACE MOORE
IN THE LATE THIRTIES.

ADVERTISEMENT FOR
BITTER SWEET ('40).

IN *I MARRIED
AN ANGEL* ('4

AS A MEMBER OF THE
AMERICAN WOMEN'S
VOLUNTARY SERVICES.

After the filming was completed, it was discovered that some scenes would have to be reshot. By this time Gable had shaved off his moustache. This obstacle was overcome by the makeup department, which supplied him with a false one. Well and good. Gable and Jeanette proceeded to the sound stage to reshoot a close-up that concludes with their kissing. They rehearsed the scene, each careful not to disturb the other's facial makeup. Then the actual take was made. When the scene was completed, Van Dyke shouted, "Cut." The two stars broke from their embrace. Only then did Jeanette discover that part of Gable's moustache was now attached to her face.

San Francisco, with its monumental twenty-minute earthquake sequence which cleansed the city, was a magnificent success. The film grossed over $6,000,000, $2,000,000 of which was profit. It was nominated for six Academy Awards (including Van Dyke's direction), and won one for Douglas Shearer's sound recording. *San Francisco* was named one of the top ten films of 1936 by *Film Daily* and was awarded the *Photoplay* magazine Gold Medal Award as Best Picture of the Year, the second time a Jeanette MacDonald film was to be so honored.

For the most part, reviewers were ecstatic. The definitive positive review was rendered by Frank S. Nugent of the *New York Times.*

> *San Francisco* . . . manages to encompass most of the virtues of the operatic film—romantic, the biographical, the dramatic and the documentary. Astonishingly, it serves all of them abundantly well . . . truly meriting commendation as a near-perfect illustration of the Cinema's inherent and acquired ability to absorb and digest other art forms and convert them into its own sinews.
>
> Especially is this true of the picture's handling of the entrancing musical sequences arranged for the lyric soprano voice of Jeanette MacDonald. Woven gracefully into the script, rather than patched over it to conceal gaps in the story fabric, they are an integral, as well as a delightful, part of the film.

It is only fair to note that there was some negative response to the project. This connotes the disparate reception to Jeanette MacDonald the performer. There were those (like the *New York Times*) who adored her, but a group felt the MacDonald-Eddy films in general, and *San Francisco* in particular, were too moralistic and even pretentious. *Time* magazine's critique was a case in point. *San Francisco,* according to that journal, offers "two unusual phenomena: the San Francisco earthquake and Jeanette MacDonald acting with her teeth. Of the two, the latter is the more appalling. The earthquake, however, has more noteworthy sound effects."

If Jeanette felt a need to prove herself a capable star without Nelson Eddy or the actual operetta format, she had done so, in most eyes. The song "San Francisco," by Gus Kahn and Bronislau Kaper, would become an enduring standard, seemingly forever associated with Miss MacDonald. Perhaps in another attempt to show she could solo star, Jeanette was heard on the "Lux Radio Theatre" on June 29, 1936 in *Irene,* the musical comedy she had appeared in years before in a small role.

While Allan Jones and Irene Dunne were on the Universal lot making *Show Boat,* Jeanette was being reteamed with Nelson Eddy in *Maytime.* It was based on the Rida Johnson Young and Sigmund Romberg operetta that had debuted on Broadway in August, 1917, for a 492-performance run. B. P. Schulberg's Preferred Pictures produced a silent version of the work in 1923 with Ethel Shannon and Harrison Ford, featuring a young Clara Bow. Irving Thalberg thought the work perfect for Jeanette, who was by then number nine of the top ten box-office attractions throughout America. Her dollar value was uplifted largely by *San Francisco,* but it was time to return to the operetta format and to waiting Nelson Eddy. Paul Lukas and Frank Morgan were contracted to support the starring team, and Jeanette's first full Technicolor production began in 1936 under the direction of Edmund Goulding.

But the world at M-G-M shook considerably on September 14, 1936, when Irving Thalberg died. Production on *Maytime* was halted until Mayer and company could achieve a balance. The conservative Mayer had battled with Thalberg because of the "immoral" content of *Maytime.* Louis B., who had one set of standards for himself and another for the world, thought it inappropriate that two emerging and sympathetic screen titans like MacDonald and Eddy should be secretly in love with each other—in the plot, that is—although married to somebody else.

Mayer finally decided to scrap the entire first *Maytime*, and film it again in black and white. Hunt Stromberg was handed the reins of production, and Edmund Goulding, Paul Lukas and Fran Morgan were replaced by director Robert Z. Leonard and actors John Barrymore and Herman Bing. There seems to be little justification for this costly move, unless Mayer simply wanted to start fresh, and ignore the value of the participants in the first version of the operetta.

In any case, not only did the director and co-starred actors find themselves replaced (some due to overlapping production schedules), but so were several lesser actors, as well as songs, costumes, and even character names. The script was revamped to Mayer's specifications.

A cast, with roles played in the first *Maytime*, follows, with notations of changes:

Peggy Van Dyck (Marcia Mornay)	Jeanette MacDonald
Richard Wayne (Paul Allison)	Nelson Eddy
Gregory Nazaroff (Nicholai Nazaroff)	Paul Lukas (John Barrymore)
Young Girl (Barbara)	Margaret Hobart (Lynne Carver)
Her Boyfriend (Kip)	Ed Anthony (Tom Brown)
Alice Pomeroy Wayne (Richard Wayne's wife—eliminated from the second *Maytime*)	Julie Hayden
Matthew Fuller (eliminated from the second *Maytime*)	Frank Morgan
Rose (Ellen)	Rafael Ottiano

Eddy's character underwent a name change to provide a cleaner-sounding surname, while in Jeanette's case, the new name tag "Marcia

93

Mornay" was in keeping with the traditional "M" or "N" she liked to have in all her character names.

Maytime was the fifty-eighth feature for director Robert Z. Leonard and he immediately established an affinity with his leading players. The fact that he had formerly performed in operettas and was a musical talent in his own right served him well.

On the set of *Maytime* one day, Leonard set out his four requisites for acting success. First, the person had to possess an ability to react naturally to situations. Second, physical beauty was necessary. Third, one had to have the intelligence to acquire technique. Fourth, it was essential to have the necessary experience to perfect the above.

Some in the cast had the most important qualifications from the above, like John Barrymore and Jeanette. But for others, such as Nelson Eddy, acting must have been a chore.

Although Leonard was sympathetic to the needs of his stars, he was not about to put up with a prima donna or the swaying temperament of an aging Barrymore. Leonard explained, "Temperament has gone out of style. . . . Most of the players are like Miss MacDonald and Eddy, hard and willing workers, who realize that harmonious working relations are essential to modern picture production." Obviously Leonard was no tiger like Van Dyke, but he knew how to handle people, or so it appeared.

Jeanette had her own way of handling co-players who got out of line. She had profited from her experiences with Maurice Chevalier, not only in avoiding his wandering hands, but in the knack of turning a fellow performer's back to the camera, so the lens will be on the proper star. The latter choreography was reserved for Mr. Eddy; the former gyration for Mr. Barrymore. It seemed that Barrymore not only had a drinking and memory problem (he used large-sized cue cards out of camera range), but he had a penchant for resting his fingers on a lady's private parts. It so happened that during the opening scenes at Louis Napoleon's palace reception, she was wearing a wide-skirted outfit. Since the camera would not reveal what she had on underneath, Jeanette took the liberty of using lounging pants for her undergarment. Seated at the banquet table for the sequence, she soon discovered that Barrymore had caught on to her clothes ploy and that her attention must be divided not only to her line cues, but to his prodding digits.

The actual production of the second *Maytime* was greatly influenced by Nelson Eddy's pending concert schedule. In a few short months, he was contracted for a tour of forty-three cities. To prevent overlapping schedules, his scenes had to be shot in succession. To speed up the process, he memorized his lines using a recorder.

One aspect of the film, a step that was taken with due deliberation, was the selection, deletion and embellishment of the music for *Maytime*. There are two firsts in this feature. *Maytime* contains the first Grand Opera music ever written (by Herbert Stothart) for the screen, and features Jeanette and Nelson singing a classic American folk song, "Carry Me Back to Old Virginny," which pre-dates the Civil War by many years.

Herbert Stothart created a Tchaikovsky opera from the Russian composer's Fifth Symphony. He arranged it as an interlude, using melodic themes and other parts for *Maytime*'s Cossack March scene and Grand Finale. Stothart explained the reasons behind his unique use of Tchaikovsky's symphony. "There are many symphonies full of grand melodic strains and perfectly adaptable to opera. And in the future these will furnish a vast field of operatic literature for the screen." An unspoken point was that the use of such virgin material prevented the public from having any unfavorable comparisons between the film's stars and real life opera performers.

The sets for the second *Maytime* were lush, as were their predecessors. Metro rebuilt a Metropolitan Opera House of 1875 on two stages, which held sixty singers and sixty-five musicians. For one part of the well-mounted picture, the palace of Louis Napoleon was created, then torn down in order to construct another imposing set, with its pieces being stored for future use. Even though *Maytime* had been altered considerably by the time director Leonard was assigned to it, he felt compelled to tear down a recently constructed cottage and garden interior/exterior because it did not express his viewpoint on the film. Such was Hollywood in its Golden Days of lavishness, waste and inspiration.

The technical director, George Richelavie, was ordered to insure that scenes and characters alike were as authentic as possible. Great care was taken with the smallest of details. For instance, Richelavie would not allow anyone to be filmed chewing gum or wearing fingernail polish or wrist watches, as none of these products existed in *Maytime*'s temporal span. He forbade the presence of small objects such as cigarettes or book matches in the tavern scenes. He explained, "Certainly they had cigarettes in those days, but they were expensive and the class of men portrayed in the particular scene wouldn't have been able to buy them." This is why productions at M-G-M, were then and are still revered throughout the film industry.

Even some of the smaller roles in *Maytime* were filled by actual opera singers. In the *Czaritza* sequence, the "shadow opera" created for the film, Kutznetzoff, a Russian basso, plays the role of the Czaritza's minister who persuades his superior to give up a young officer. Merova, a Russian contralto who for many seasons was with the Russian opera company in New York, is seen as Jeanette's companion in this ten-minute sequence.

Maytime, which would become Jeanette's favorite of all her films, had her ultimate approval in three ways. First of all, she thought it was the best all-round picture she was ever in. Second, the role of Marcia Mornay was her favorite. She explained, "Marcia answered my striving for a truly dramatic part, as the story ranged from the time she was a romantic girl all through her life until she was a magnificent grande dame of eighty, a rare opportunity for expressing varieties of feeling and character delineation." Third, *Maytime,* along with her next film, *The Firefly,* adorned her in the best costumes she ever wore on screen.

Most every filmgoer, at least in the Thirties, had a soft spot for unrequited love, death scenes and a happy ending. *Maytime* had all three elements. With the blending of Adrian's costumes, Cedric Gibbons' Third Empire settings, Oliver T. Marsh's flattering cinematography, and the telling score (thanks to Stothart, Romberg, Young, Bob Wright, Chet Forrest, James A. Bland, and Cyrus Wood), the 132 minutes of screen time float by. One has to admire the craftiness of the plotline, which finds Marcia Mornay wedding her considerate but unromantic mentor (Barrymore) at the expense of losing the man she loves, fellow American opera singer Paul Allison (Eddy). Years later at the Metropolitan Opera, Marcia and Paul are reunited for a singing engagement. Her husband suspects the truth of their feeling and in a jealous pique shoots and kills Paul. Marcia retires from the concert stage. Years later, in a tiny American town on May Day, 1906, she helps to re-tie the romance of two young lovers, who remind her of years gone by. Later that day, she dies in the garden, only to have her soul rise up and walk down the garden path with an equally spiritual

Paul. As Archer Winsten would celebrate in the *New York Post*, "[*Maytime* is] a rich melancholy tapestry of music, love and regret."

Many felt so in 1936, and cinema historians today agree that *Maytime* was the zenith of the operetta cycle in American films. In particular, the contrast of settings, moods, and music was to be commended. An indelible recurring image from the film is the well-appointed May Day fair, with Jeanette being pushed in the vine-covered swing by Eddy as flower blossoms spill through the air. It is here that the remarkably saccharine but pertinent "Will You Remember (Sweetheart)" is first sung, to be repeated in duet at the ethereal finale as the eternal lovers walk hand in hand down the road, united forever.

On the basis of *Maytime*, Jeanette and Nelson were named the "King and Queen of the Screen" by *Screen Guide* magazine. Jeanette seemed to be able to do no wrong. She appeared almost too good to be true.

But she was very human, after all. Nat W. Finston, associated with Jeanette at Paramount and later at M-G-M (where he was also head of the music department), is now residing at the Motion Picture County Home. He has sharp recollections of Jeanette of the 1930s. As he assesses it, "At Paramount, she was the sweetest, easiest thing in the world. . . . At M-G-M she got spoiled." In fact, according to him, "At M-G-M she didn't always sing as well as at Paramount. . . . The mixer would patch up everything she missed. [A typical practice then as now.] "She was difficult when she had her period. She said her voice wasn't right. . . . Very often she held up the shooting. She'd come an hour late, [sometimes] two hours late. . . . She was erratic. Very often she came and didn't know her lines."

Another surviving M-G-M executive, Sam Marx, head of the story department in the Thirties and often a producer on the lot, communicated to me when I was preparing this book:

> Miss MacDonald annoyed the hell out of me one day. I knew her when we both lived in New York—she was on West 55th Street and appeared in a Shubert work of art called *Boom Boom*. I did not appreciate the airs she assumed (nonmusical) when she became a film star.
>
> On the day I speak of, I was waiting a matter of almost

97

one hour to see Louis B. Mayer on a story department matter; he was tied up—and just as there were sounds of his becoming available, Jeanette bounced in to see him. His secretary (Jeanette Spooner) told Miss MacDonald I needed a "Yes" or "No" answer that should require about ten seconds. At that moment, Mr. Mayer's visitor came out and it was my turn. But Jeanette MacDonald jumped in front of me, asked sweetly if she could precede me because she had a hairdressing appointment and without waiting for my answer, said "I promise Sam, I won't be any more than forty-five minutes!" Then she went in.

I'm still steaming over it. . . .

CHAPTER SIX

Maytime may have been a high point in Jeanette's professional life, but it was two years earlier, in June, 1935, that her life reached romantic fruition. One evening Jeanette journeyed alone to the home of a friend, Rozika Dolly, who had invited her to a dinner party. By this time she and Bob Ritchie had parted romantic ways, but Jeanette's penchant for tardiness had not left her. There she stood, on Rozika Dolly's steps, an hour later, rehearsing a plausible apology. As fate would have it, another guest was equally late. He was a blond young man slightly reminiscent of her new co-star, Nelson Eddy, but who possessed a sterling charm all his own, which considerably aided his most successful film to date, *Zoo in Budapest.*

Jeanette knew Gene Raymond only by reputation. They stood somewhat awkwardly in front of a closed door the butler seemed to be taking his own sweet time opening. They made a futile attempt at small talk. Then the door was flung open. Rozika shrieked out, "How nice that you two came together," before the pair could make their very separate apologies.

As soon as the just-coupled Jeanette and Gene entered the drawing room, a flashbulb popped. That meant the two would be billed as a romantic twosome in next morning's paper, so, for the moment, they decided not to break anyone's illusions. In fact, when one man tried to steal Jeanette for the first dance after dinner, Gene, the gallant "escort," would not hear of it.

They danced together for the first time that evening, still calling

99

each other "Mr." and "Miss." Years later, candid Jeanette admitted, with a lilting laughter to her voice, "Gene's attentions were on another lady that night. . . . I thought he hardly noticed me."

Their second meeting was at another door. This time it was the entrance to a lawyer's office who just happened to be representing them —separately, of course. It had been some two weeks since they had met on Rozika's doorsteps, and Gene considered it presumptuous to follow through on a relationship started accidentally.

A few days later there was an important premiere at Grauman's Chinese Theatre in Hollywood. Both Jeanette and Gene enjoyed extremely cordial relationships with their mothers (some were less kind in describing Raymond's very possessive, doting mama). Coincidentally, each family decided to attend the show. As fate would have it, Gene also was a latecomer, and both arrived at the event about half an hour after the other stars showed up. By then gawkers had thinned out. MacDonald and Raymond bumped into one another, and photographers anxiously asked them to pose for pictures.

The foursome sat together at the premiere, and afterward went to Brown's for sodas. Gene must have felt by this time he and Jeanette were well enough acquainted to go out on a real date. He asked her to go dancing with him the next evening. Gene is reported to have ventured, "Since everyone has us in love, don't you think we should at least have one date so everyone won't be wrong?" Jeanette agreed.

On Monday, June 17, Gene and Jeanette started on the road to sweetheartdom. There is some conflict as to where they went on the date. Some insist Gene took her to the Cocoanut Grove Club for dinner. Others argue they were going to dine there, but vetoed it due to the incredible publicity that had built up around their new relationship, and instead dined at Jeanette's home.

It is likely the pair dined at the MacDonald residence, as both were basically loners, and desired their private lives to be just that, private. Of course, Anna MacDonald was there to chaperone the two.

According to the subjects, the evening was something less than smashing. Jeanette and Gene could not really think of much to say to each other, and Mrs. MacDonald, a good conversationalist, could not break the wall of formality between her daughter and her date.

To sound one another out, the couple exchanged the stories of their lives. Jeanette learned that he was born in Brooklyn, a Leo (Au-

100

gust 13, 1908—she was a Gemini), that his mother (Mary Smith Guion) was positive her son was destined for a theatrical career, and that he made his first stage appearance at age five. His parents had enrolled him in Manhattan's Professional Children's School and he made his Broadway debut in March, 1920, in *The Piper*. Jeanette and her mother must have exchanged knowing looks, recalling her experiences in *The Night Boat* at that very time.

Gene had had a succession of Broadway roles throughout the Twenties, playing in such shows as *Why Not, The Potters, Cradle Snatchers* (with Humphrey Bogart and Raymond Hackett), *Take My Advice,* a revival of *Sherlock Holmes, The War Song,* and *Jonesy.* Raymond admitted sheepishly that it was when he was with Paramount Pictures in 1930 that his surname was changed. He confessed he appreciated the chance to get rid of a "difficult handle." Jeanette had to laugh. Her reserve was breaking down.

Gene and Jeanette, who had seen each other at Paramount during the early Thirties but had traveled in different social and business circles, each had their impressions to share of the studio and of Jesse L. Lasky who had had such faith in both of them. Raymond had a sense of humor about how Hollywood had tried to promote him as the platinum blond leading man and about his two experiences to date at M-G-M. First he had been Clark Gable's rival for chipper Jean Harlow in *Red Dust,* and then two years later, in 1934, he had been persuaded to accept the "heel" role in Joan Crawford's *Sadie McKee.* He had fought against doing the film—Franchot Tone and Edward Arnold had showier roles—but he had to admit, the picture had made quite an impression with the public and had done his career good.

As he related his story, Jeanette began to sense the depth of character behind the facade of the conventional handsome leading man. She plied him with questions about the musicals he was making with Ann Sothern at RKO and wondered how co-workers responded to opera prima donna Lily Pons, then at Gene's studio. He said he would soon know. His bosses had informed him they were to be teamed for a project entitled *That Girl from Paris.* He was to play a jazz band leader. That was a laugh.

But the stiffness of propriety never left the evening. It did not help matters that Jeanette served eggplant and Gene hated eggplant. Yet that first night, Gene did not complain about anything. When he departed about 10:30, Jeanette thought, "How could I have been such a poor hostess?" She was certain she had seen the last of him. For his part, on the way home, Gene was asking himself, "How could I have been such a poor guest?"

All was not lost, however. The next morning he called and invited her to the Trocadero Club. That evening they danced frequently together. But it did not seem to be a smooth date, for after ten P.M., Jeanette began ask Gene the time every fifteen minutes. He was convinced she must be totally bored.

But at one minute after midnight, Jeanette confided to Gene, "Yesterday was my birthday. Now, let's dance."

Their third date took them to the races. Since they both adored horses, they went to the track often. The opera and horse shows were two other favorite pastimes for the couple.

Although Jeanette had dated Nelson Eddy, James Stewart, and Henry Fonda during the time of *Naughty Marietta*'s triumph, that was largely for publicity sake. She was seen more and more frequently with Gene. He was with her when her prize Skye terrior, "Stormy Weather," won a Blue Ribbon at a dog show. He threw her a surprise *Rose-Marie* birthday party in 1936, with the men coming as Royal Canadian Mounted Police and the women as Rose-Maries.

Some forty years later, scenarist, playwright, authoress and wit Anita Loos recalled for me, "Jeanette was such a private person, there is little to report on her activities at M-G-M." But there was no doubt for Miss Loos or others on the Metro lot about Jeanette's feelings for Gene. Nat W. Finston recalls seeing them frequently on the Metro spread walking hand-in-hand.

On Thursday, August 13, 1936, just about a month before thirty-six-year old Irving Thalberg died, Gene proposed to Jeanette. The setting for the occasion was the famed Mission Inn in Riverside, California. Before lunch, Gene drove Jeanette up the tortuous road to the top of Mount Rubidoux and there he asked the important question. She accepted.

But the career still came first. Jeanette was enmeshed in the making of *Maytime* (both versions). On September 19, 1936, she was in the recording studio dueting "Indian Love Call" and "Ah, Sweet Mystery of Life" with Nelson Eddy, and two days later, the couple were making Victor recordings of "Farewell to Dreams" and "Will You

102

Remember (Sweetheart)," both from *Maytime*. The duo also recorded "Song of Love" from *Blossom Time,* but the session was declared not up to par, and the cut was shelved. It was to be Jeanette's last official recording session for three years.

In January, 1937, Jeanette was voted the best female singer on the screen by a *Modern Screen* magazine poll, with partner Nelson Eddy as best male singer. Fredric March was voted best actor, M-G-M's Robert Taylor the most handsome male star, Loretta Young the most beautiful actress, Fred Astaire and (M-G-M's) Eleanor Powell were best screen dancers, and Jeanette's friend Norma Shearer was named the screen's best actress.

On January 25, 1937, Jeanette was heard again on the "Lux Radio Theatre," this time starring in *Tonight or Never,* a prior Gloria Swanson film. The picture's original co-star, Melvyn Douglas, was Jeanette's vis-à-vis. For a time, Jeanette would have a radio series on ABC network, which provided an attractive $5,000 weekly salary.

By this time, Jeanette's sister Blossom had come to the West coast to find her fortune in Hollywood. When vaudeville had died, she and her husband (Warren Rock) had switched into legitimate acting. The Rocks toured in *Grand Hotel* and other shows together. Blossom won acclaim playing a whore in Sidney Kingsley's Pulitzer Prize-winning play, *Dead End,* in 1936. An M-G-M talent scout spotted her, and probably with Jeanette's influence, signed Blossom to a studio contract. (Nepotism was nothing unique on the Hollywood lots, whether among executive staffs or acting talent. At Culver City, Norma Shearer's brother, reputed to be tone deaf, was head of the sound department, while young Mickey Rooney's vaudevillian father, Joe Yule, had a minor player's contract at the studio.) Blossom made her debut in 1937 at M-G-M under a new acting name "Marie Blake" in *Mannequin,* starring Joan Crawford and Spencer Tracy. In 1938 Marie would achieve some measure of success through being cast in the regular role of Sally, the big-mouthed switchboard operator in the *Dr. Kildare* series with Lew Ayres.

By 1937 the only immediate member of the successful Mac-Donald family not in California was the oldest sister Elsie, who was running an acting and dancing school in Philadelphia.

Jeanette undertook a concert tour in early spring of 1937, but it was not long before the marriage bells would ring. Her publicist, Helen

Ferguson, gave Jeanette a bridal shower, and so did Helen's mother Emilie. Friends such as Inez Courtney, Irene Dunne, Irene Hervey (who would marry Allan Jones), Shirley Ross, Mary Brian (who had dated Gene in the Paramount days) and Anita Louise attended these affairs. It was an exciting time for Jeanette, allowing her to be girlish and to enjoy all the attention, well wishes and pampering that is bestowed on a forthcoming bride. How different from her clandestine relationship with Bob Ritchie!

While Jeanette was busy being showered, touring and even starting preproduction on a new film, *The Firefly, sans* Nelson Eddy, Gene was preoccupied not only with his active career, but with furnishing a house he had secretly purchased for himself and his bride. It took him six months to furnish the home they would call "Twin Gables," a five-acre property that rested on the top of a hill. Jeanette, usually so perspicacious, claimed she never suspected a thing. She did wonder aloud why Gene found something wrong with every house they looked at together. Could he be getting cold feet?

If Gene was *not* uncertain about his love for Jeanette, Mrs. Guion was. Despite the passing of four decades, Allan Jones today has no difficulty remembering how she felt about the situation. "I'm sure that for her, no girl was good enough for Gene . . . she was very possessive."

Tragedy had its special way of impinging upon the couple's pending bliss. Deaths always came in threes in Hollywood and so it did on the M-G-M lot. John Gilbert, once the pride of the studio, died at age thirty-eight on January 9, 1936, by himself and drunk. On September 14, 1936, Irving Thalberg had passed away, and many felt it was the beginning of the downward path for M-G-M. Then on Monday, June 7, 1937, twenty-six-year-old Jean Harlow died. Her sudden, inexplicable illness—never fully explained—was a shock to everyone at the Culver City facilities. While Jeanette and Jean had never been close friends, they were well acquainted. Their star bungalows on the lot were not far apart. On June 9 the funeral was held at the Wee Kirk of the Heather at Forest Lawn Cemetery in Glendale. There were 250 invited guests. Mrs. Genevieve Smith, a Christian Science Reader, conducted the service. Although it had been Grace Moore who tearfully sang the Psalm of David at Thalberg's funeral, here Jeanette was asked to sing —of all things—"Indian Love Call," while Nelson Eddy ended the service with a rendition of "Ah, Sweet Mystery of Life."

Exactly a week later Jeanette and Gene were married. The date of their wedding may have been a rather spontaneous choice. Very early one morning, Jeanette and Gene telephoned Rosamond Rice, a clerk, to register an application for marriage. Since each had to be on the set early every day, it was impossible for them to call during regular business hours. Rice got out of bed to fulfill their request.

Originally the preferred date for the nuptials was June 17, the anniversary of their first date. This proved impossible because the needed church was booked for that day, so they chose Wednesday, June 16, 1937.

Naturally the wedding plans had to be processed and approved of by Louis B. Mayer. Knowing Jeanette's stern will, he realized there was little chance of dissuading one half of the lucrative love team of MacDonald and Eddy from postponing the ceremony. The short, aging Jewish man must have envied Gene Raymond his good luck. Adopting a paternalistic air, and thankful for some legitimate occasion to help gloss over the Harlow death and funeral, he gave his blessing.

Three hundred guests were invited to the ceremony at the Wilshire Methodist Church. The occasion was reputed to cost approximately $25,000 and would rank in Hollywood history as the most lavish wedding since Vilma Banky and Rod La Roque had married in the Twenties.

Among the distinguished wedding party were Nelson Eddy, Allan Jones, Mary Pickford and Charles "Buddy" Rogers, the Dick Hargreaves (Helen Ferguson), Warren Rock and Marie Blake, Robert Marlow (Gene's brother), Fay Wray, Harold Lloyd, Mr. and Mrs. Johnny Mack Brown and the Basil Rathbones. Louis B. Mayer organized the occasion.

Jeanette was given away by her mother, Anna MacDonald. Bridal attendants were Fay Wray, Ginger Rogers, Marie, Helen Ferguson and Mrs. Johnny Mack Brown. Robert Marlow was the best man. Harold Lloyd, Allan Jones, Johnny Mack Brown, Basil Rathbone, Richard Hargreaves and Warren Rock were ushers.

The ceremony, officiated at by the Reverend Willsie Martin, was scheduled to begin at nine P.M., but actually did not start until 9:40. The cool summer night featured a fresh breeze which stirred the hair and twisted the imagination of the hundreds of onlookers who "oohed" and "ahhed" every time another celebrity entered the church. The full

105

moon rose high that night, allowing everyone to witness the spectacle. The crowds became so intense the police had to rope off the area. But even one hundred police were incapable of containing spontaneous applause which rang out at the slightest hint of the privileged goings-on inside.

One person who did *not* attend the festivities was Gene's mother. Among her complaints about Jeanette was that Miss MacDonald was a "cradle snatcher." Her son was only twenty-eight, and Jeanette was anywhere from one to five years older than Raymond (Actually, two days after the ceremony, Jeanette would be thirty-four years old.) Over the years a rumor has built up that Gene's mother stood outside the church picketing the wedding, but this is denied by those who attended the affair.

The service began with Nelson Eddy singing "I Love You Truly," and later "Oh Perfect Love." During the intonation of the Lord's Prayer an unexplained explosion was heard outside the church, but may have been the crowd cheering. Upon the striking of the chords to Lohengrin's Wedding March, the bridesmaids drifted in, followed by Jeanette, who at no time looked anywhere but straight ahead. Among those standing in the pews, marveling at how much Jeanette had accomplished over the years, was the star's best friend from Philadelphia high-school days, Margaret Watson.

Jeanette was radiantly lovely in a gown of flesh pink, her favorite color, over a delicate pink taffeta with a lace collar. The dress had a redingote top with long, full sleeves, and was flowing to the floor, and extended with a lush train. The veil was of pink tulle. From a shell-shaped lace cap, a short veil extended over the tulle, and the cap was edged with delicate flowers. Jeanette carried a gold-embroidered pink satin prayer book with the initials "J" and "G" embossed in the corner.

The bride and groom's voices were loud and definite as they took their vows. With the completion of the ceremony, Jeanette and Gene turned to walk down the aisle. Friends and relatives beamed, while the husband and wife looked straight ahead. They were momentarily prevented from leaving by their guests. The ushers ran around trying to clear the aisle. Allan Jones was a bit embarrassed because his shoes squeaked. Nobody noticed.

Everyone started snatching roses from the floral decorations. Mary Pickford plucked one and put it in husband Buddy Rogers' lapel. The wedding pair finally emerged from the church, and with the yelling crowds held back, they made their exit in a waiting limousine.

Because of filming commitments, the couple had to postpone their honeymoon. Instead they settled for a reception at Jeanette's home. The only reporter to attend the ceremony had been Louella Parsons. Jeanette had been firm that there was to be nothing "commercial" about the ceremony, no newsmen scurrying to and fro, no photographers rushing about to snap candid shots.

But crafty Louella was not to be outdone. She tucked a portable typewriter under her silver fox cape and when she reached the MacDonald home she went directly to the powder room, locked the door, and started pecking out her exclusive scoop.

As Miss Parsons would recall it, "Suddenly there was a knock at the door. And the bride called, 'Louella, you and that typewriter come right out here.' And when I came out, sheepishly, I found a table set up for me. A telephone at my elbow, a glass of champagne and a piece of wedding cake. 'You might as well work in comfort,' laughed the lovely Jeanette, 'You're going to do it anyway!'"

Following the festive reception, Gene escorted his bride to their new home, Twin Gables on the Claudell Estate in Bel Air. She was enchanted by the surprise. The next day found Jeanette back at M-G-M to complete *The Firefly*.

It was not until Saturday, June 26 that the couple embarked on their honeymoon trip. They boarded the liner *Lurline* to Honolulu. Other passengers on the ship included Mary Pickford and her new husband, Buddy Rogers. The Raymonds vacationed in a cottage on the north side of Oahu. They did not separate until 1938, when Gene went on a personal appearance tour.

CHAPTER SEVEN

Nothing is more difficult to accept than the shattering of self-delusions. Movie fans around the world had been convinced that the romancing of Jeanette and Nelson Eddy on camera was duplicated off screen. It was a jolt for many to accept the marriage of Jeanette to Gene Raymond. In fact, even two years later when Nelson wed Anne Daniels, the public became aghast and confused all over again. How could Eddy wed another, when he must certainly be in love with his lovely cinema leading lady!

The public was even more baffled when it was learned that Jeanette's newest film, *The Firefly,* would not co-star her with Nelson Eddy, but with Allan Jones. This situation came about because independent Jeanette did not want to be labeled one half of a team, but a self-sufficient star. Producer Hunt Stromberg supported her in the campaign to make Jones her leading man in this venture. Even Mayer had to agree that the role of "Don Diego" the dashing spy during the Napoleonic Wars would be incongruous if played by the rather stiff and wooden Mr. Eddy. So it was official, Jones would join Jeanette in the Rudolf Friml operetta (vastly rewritten), while Nelson would be matched with Ilona Massey in Cole Porter's *Rosalie.* It was no secret around Hollywood that Miss Massey had been contracted by Metro as insurance in case the newly married Mrs. Raymond got too uppity in her demands.

To prepare for her role of "Nina Maria," the Spanish dancer who engages in espionage, Jeanette studied four-and-one-half hours daily for

109

one month with her old dancing teacher, Albertina Rasch. This is where the years of strenuous dance practice paid dividends for Jeanette. After limbering up exercises, she could execute Spanish dances at difficult tempos, skillfully interweaving the bolero, tango, fandango, and flamenco, as she switched partners.

Jeanette was surprised by many people's bewilderment at why she worked so hard while a top star. She explained, "The minute you let yourself ride along on the wave just because people around you are telling you how wonderful you are, you're sunk."

The venerable Rudolf Friml arrived on the scene while the script was being prepared (and retailored to specifications), and worked with the musical director to adapt the operatic sequences in coordination with the scenario.

Jeanette and designer Adrian scrupulously examined the twenty-five costumes she was to wear in *The Firefly*, but final approval was in the hands of director Robert Z. Leonard. One costume used over 150 yards of lace, which was hand-spangled in minute sequins, and the lace traced in seed pearls. Allan Jones was featured in two types of costumes —first, "civilian" clothes consisting of a bolero jacket, knee breeches, cape, buckled shoes, and Spanish sombrero. He also wore the uniform of a Captain of French Hussars. In the riding sequences, Jones sported high leather boots, and traveled on his own thoroughbred horse, "Smokey."

Even the makeup was very special. M-G-M made a big publicity gimmick out of having to secure government permission to highlight Jeanette's face with a gold powder, allegedly worth a fortune. The makeup was composed of gold dust mixed with flour. It was an impalpable powder, the finest possible. The fine grains left a yellowish glow to Jeanette's face. The composition was mixed with grease paint by makeup man Jack Dawn. The result was a satin-type finish which absorbed only half of the light of ordinary makeup.

Since Spain in 1937 was engulfed in a Civil War, M-G-M had to look elsewhere to authenticate the various facets of the production. The studio's Paris office came to the rescue on some details. Background musicians were located in Mexico City by Herbert Stothart, who brought famous guitarist Manuel Alvarez Maciste to Hollywood, as well as others.

Crafty Robert Z. Leonard sent to a Los Angeles department store for a complete set of lead toy soldiers, in order to make a miniature of the Battle of Vittoria, fought by France, Spain and England. In reality, *The Firefly* was shot on thirty major sets, using some five hundred extras.

The two major outdoor locations for the film were in the Lone Pine Mountains. The sixty-person trek to the foot of the High Sierras was accompanied by a stage coach, four mules, a donkey cart, donkeys, a trailer for Jones' horse "Smokey" and twelve truckloads of equipment.

The treacherous nature of this brand of film production should be appreciated. Allan Jones came away from *The Firefly* knowing full well the obstacles of making motion pictures in the mountains.

One morning during filming, everyone arose at 4:30 A.M. and took the usual half hour to prepare for the journey by truck, bus and mule to the shooting site. Upon reaching the spot, the crew, already with several days' practice, hid the telltale equipment behind boulders and between crags, and the narrow roadways were watched by California police to prevent motorists from straying onto the locale. Between huge boulders a construction unit had built a wall to simulate Pyrenees mountain roads, with their protective outer edge.

A stagecoach sat, containing the several characters with whom Don Diego (Jones) was to exchange dialogue after trotting up to the coach. As a signal for the sequence to start, Leonard was to fire one shot, which meant get ready, and two shots, which meant to start. He did so. Jones smoothly rode up to the carriage, and greeted the riders. Leonard then yelled, "That's it, that's it, hold it for a test, Allan. Now we've got to get the shot of the mules pulling out of there and you riding alongside."

The mules then balked and Jones found himself caught between the coach and the wall. Although an excellent horseman, Jones could not extricate himself from the situation. He was being slowly crushed between two seemingly immovable objects. One toe was completely protruding from his riding boot, and his foot scraped the rough wall. Finally, the coach toppled over, and Jones was freed. The women were quickly pulled out, and company manager Frank Messenger crawled under the coach to spot the damage. "One of the braces has snapped," he told Leonard. "Get me some two-by-fours. We'll have to jack it up."

While the crew was putting the coach back into shape, nurse Dorothy Smith soaked Jones' swelling foot in hot water obtained from

111

the commissary wagon. Dr. Howard W. Dueker happily told Jones he only had a sprain, and when the scene was reshot, the star refused to allow a bit player to double for him.

Yet Jones' recollection of the filming of *The Firefly* is not of pain, but of pleasure. Even today he beams as he reconstructs the opening day of shooting on the picture. Jeanette walked over to her favorite cameraman, Oliver T. Marsh, and said, "Ollie, Allan and I are co-stars. He is to get equal treatment. Everything you do for me, do for him . . . he is to get the same number of close-ups."

Jeanette, ever more interested in the overall quality of the production rather than herself being dramatically showcased, practically handed the film to Jones on a platter.* While many of the songs from the original Friml-Harbach score were left intact ("Giannina Mia," "Sympathy" and "Love Is Like a Firefly"), it was decided the film required a new specialty number. From one of Friml's piano works, Metro composers Chet Forrest and Bob Wright created "The Donkey Serenade" as a solo for Jones. It proved to be the hit of the picture and Jeanette would not hear of its being shortened or deleted at Allan's expense. (It would become Jones' trademark song. Strangely, Jeanette would later record a version of this traditionally man's number.)

The Firefly, filmed in impressive Sepiatone, proved that Jeanette could handle a picture on her own, all 131 minutes' worth. But it was not quite the success of her three joint efforts with Nelson Eddy. There was a division of opinion as to Jeanette's performance. Some felt she was definitely being too coy and arch as she batted her eyelashes and sashayed about the slow-moving costumed spy drama. John T. McManus *(New York Times)* remarked that she "is neither actress nor dancer enough to be asked to do all the dissembling and dervishing [required of her]. . . ." On the other hand, the more gentle *Variety* (who depended on M-G-M advertisement even more than the *Times*) countered that *The Firefly* was "a triumph for Jeanette MacDonald, who sings and dances brilliantly. . . . In voice and appearance she is as lovely to listen to and look upon as she was in *Naughty Marietta* and *Maytime*, when she appeared with Nelson Eddy. . . . To her unquestioned photo-

---

*Upon the completion of *The Firefly* producer Stromberg presented Jeanette with a silver plate etched with a scene from the film. Upon her death, she willed it to Allan Jones.

112

graphic and musical talents, she displays added versatility . . . as a graceful and skillful dancer." There were also those reviewers who politely suggested that perhaps Jeanette was now a bit too "mature" to play such a youthful, agile heroine and that she should realize she was acting in a motion picture and not a filmed grand opera.

During the filming of *The Firefly* director Leonard had carried over one of the jokes used by Jeanette's favorite, W. S. Van Dyke. Before she and Jones were about to launch into a duet for the cameras (which had been prerecorded), he quieted the set for a playback of the duet. Suddenly over the loudspeakers blared forth the dulcet tones of Jeanette and *Nelson Eddy*. The cast broke up in glee.

But Nelson Eddy was *not* laughing. If he had been wary of Allan Jones during the making of *Rose-Marie*, he was hypersensitive at this point of the rivalry. While his *Rosalie* had been a satisfying bit of entertainment—some said thanks to the Cole Porter score and the joint presence of Eleanor Powell and Ilona Massey—he was worried about the future. During the course of shooting *The Firefly* and afterward, he subtly and in other ways informed Louis B. Mayer and studio manager Eddie Mannix that this was to be the first and last MacDonald-Jones joint film or else.

Why would Mayer accede to such blandishments from Eddy? Jeanette had openly stated she had never enjoyed making a film more and that she never had liked a co-star better than Jones. (Third *Firefly* lead Warren William, while congenial and polished as an urbane performer, remained aloof from everyone on the set.) There were three factors contributing to the situation and Mayer's policy decision.

Ever since Ida Koverman had persuaded Mayer of Nelson Eddy's array of talents, he had been a great booster of the baritone. The box-office receipts had substantiated this faith. On the other hand, he had never enjoyed a cordial relationship with Allan Jones, who was too independent and too unsubservient. Before long, neither employer nor employee would be speaking to one another, and Jones would be forced to sit out the balance of his M-G-M tenure, benched as spiteful punishment. Thirdly, mercurial Mayer had increasingly come to believe that Jeanette had transferred to M-G-M only at the entreaties of her friend Thalberg. According to Mayer's way of twisted thinking, any ally of the late producer was no trusted pal of the supreme boss. Confirming this growing breach between sensitive mogul and star was Jeanette's insistence that she should always re-record her soundtracks for the French film versions of her pictures. For reasons that have yet to be uncovered, Mayer was against this practice. When Jeanette maneuvered behind his back to continue this practice on *The Firefly*, Mayer's wrath was tremendous. However, he was a businessman first and a vindictive tyrant second (at least, usually in that order). For the time being, he controlled his anger. Jeanette was too valuable to the array of M-G-M stars. She was earning "the top half of a million dollars a year" and the studio had too much invested in her to consider letting her go. Metro had lost Deanna Durbin to Universal, the mistake of a decade, Mayer insisted. True, M-G-M had the services of equally young Judy Garland but she was still an unproven star talent. Thus Jeanette had to be pampered, but there was no reason why she could not be controlled. She and Eddy would just have to squash their self-esteem and make more films together.

If ever Hollywood spawned an ideal marriage, it was that of Jeanette and Gene Raymond. No fan magazine could have fabricated a more suitable union. It is one of the true great love stories of the twentieth century.

A truce of sorts had been established between Gene's mother and Jeanette and now the couple set about completing the decorations of their joint household. They had Twin Gables painted beige with dusty rose woodwork, covering over the original natural stone. M-G-M's premier singing star tried her darndest to become domestic, especially in the cooking department.

Yet, with no malice intended, she continued to serve dishes Gene did not like. For instance, she enjoyed rabbit and used to feed it to him under the guise of chicken. One evening, the jig was up. After dining on rabbit à la incognito, Jeanette impishly asked her husband his opinion of the cuisine. He replied with mock solemnity. "Do you think we could have real chicken next time?" On the other hand, she was quite adept at turning out specialties, among them Boston baked beans

114

and desserts. Scenarist DeWitt Bodeen, a good friend of Jeanette's over the years, recalls that she was a whiz at making "delicious little individual chocolate meringues."

Jeanette always called Gene "Pappy" or "Old Man Raymond," and he, in turn, would refer to her as "Jam" (a carryover from her childhood days). At other times he referred to her as "Bunko," but for the life of him (or Jeanette) he could never remember where that term of endearment had originated.

As before she wed, Jeanette disliked socializing at cocktail parties. Not only did she not drink (milk was her favorite liquid), but she felt work and career should be separated, and most such gatherings turned into business sessions. She mingled after hours with relatively few show-business folk. Besides Norma Shearer, Allan Jones and Nelson Eddy on the Metro lot, her film friends included Colleen Moore, director Tay Garnett, Otto Kruger and his wife, the Jean Hersholts and composer-conductor David Rose.

On those occasions when Jeanette and Gene did entertain, she carried through a custom she had begun years before of having each invitee sign a guest book. (She was furious to discover that on one occasion someone had ripped out two pages from the register, obviously bent on collecting famous autographs.)

While Jeanette and Gene grew further apart from his mother (he came to marvel at how Jeanette tolerated the barbs thrust at her, and began to refer to his parent's affection as "smother love"), the Raymonds developed a close bond with the MacDonald clan. Through the years Gene would remain very attached to Anna, Blossom and Elsie.

Marie Blake, as Blossom was now called, for years loved to recall the party she and her husband hosted not long after the Raymonds wed. "We gave a party called 'Come as You Think You'll Look in Fifty Years.' Jeanette and Gene came. M-G-M had made them up, and when they came to the door, I didn't recognize them. I thought they were just two old people who had stopped by. It was great fun. I went as the perennial ingenue with one foot in the grave. Attached to my ankle was a tombstone with an original poem which read,

> *As Blossom MacDonald she started life,*
> *As Blossom Rock she became a wife.*

115

For her movie career she was tagged Marie Blake.
The studio told her to jump in the lake.
P.S. She did!

Jeanette urged that Allan Jones be at least considered for the role of the outlaw Ramerez in her next project, *The Girl of the Golden West*, slated for a March, 1938, release. But Mayer refused. With Miss MacDonald as Mary Robbins, a saloon owner who falls in love with a desperado, Metro cast Nelson Eddy. He was to play the sly Lieutenant Johnson who masquerades as the bandito.

Jeanette was especially attracted to this project because it allowed her to play a rough-and-ready frontier woman. It was a wonderful opportunity to get away from the porcelain doll of *Naughty Marietta*. As Mary Robbins, she would ride a horse, stomp around the saloon setting, and sport an almost non-made-up look. Indeed, she looked forward to portraying this unsophisticated, almost unladylike girl.

Two years of research went into the project, but nothing could seemingly elevate the worn-out melodrama based on David Belasco's 1905 stage hit. It proved to be Jeanette's least successful film until the aborted version of *I Married an Angel* in 1942. Filmed in Sepia under the guidance of Robert Z. Leonard, no effort was spared to reproduce the period costumes, or to have authenticity in the diction of the multi-origin cast.

The Polka saloon owned by Mary in the story was a particularly interesting re-created artifact. Heavy timbers were plastered and pegged together with wooden bits. Door hinges were made of rawhide. Signs like "Letters Wrote Cirreckt and Legible—Condolences, $1; Business, $5; Pussinal and Love, $10 and up" could be spotted around the set. Between the signs were two large mounted Kodiak bears, and the walls were adorned with saddles (for sale).

There was a musical potpourri. Jeanette had occasion to vocalize "Liebestraum" (at the saloon) and "Ave Maria" (at the parish church). Eddy offered "Señorita," and together they dueted "Who Are We to

Say." But it was two hours of sluggish going. Not even the comedy song turn by Buddy Ebsen, "The West Ain't Wild Anymore," elevated the proceedings very much. As the *New York Sun* sympathized, "Jeanette MacDonald's voice, like her acting, seems continually to be improving. This cannot be said of her pictures." Allan Jones must have uttered a silent "I told you so," when reading *Time* magazine's comment on lethargic Eddy who displayed "roly-poly pinkness" as the alleged Mexican outlaw.

Fortunately, producer Hunt Stromberg provided the screen couple with a comeback of sorts in *Sweethearts,* their first modern-dress picture together. It was a Thanksgiving, 1938, release and a colorful one at that. Jeanette and Nelson play Broadway stars who become tired of performing the same hit show endlessly and break up, hoping to find success in Hollywood. But in true musical comedy tradition they are eventually reunited and wind up playing the same stage success again and again. Based on the operetta by Harry B. Smith, Fred DeGresac, Robert B. Smith and Victor Herbert, the script was updated and adapted by Alan Campbell and the notable Dorothy Parker. The acid Miss Parker later said that the combined factors of Jeanette and Nelson Eddy "were enough to turn her stomach." It indicated that everything was not always sweet-smelling in a MacDonald-Eddy production.

Sweethearts marked a reunion of Jeanette, Nelson, director Woody Van Dyke, Herbert Stothart and Frank Morgan from *Naughty Marietta.* Van Dyke liked the notion of filming the production in color. "Color," he enthused, "is perfect for the life and warmth and reality of stars like MacDonald and Eddy." One studio pundit added, "Don't overlook the fact that tints break lots of icicles off Eddy."

One of the more ambitious sets created for *Sweethearts* was the duplication of NBC's New York recording audition for Jeanette's number, "Summer Serenade." Two to three hundred extras were in the audience during the filming of that scene.

As always, there was a good deal of clowning on "One-Take" Woody's set. On-camera slips were often covered up, and others proved the source of added comedy relief in the film. Once, Nelson Eddy (who was becoming more portly each year) split his very tight pants in his attempt to avoid bumping into a series of backstage props. It had taken his valet Hans some fifteen minutes to get him into the pants. He

117

successfully covered the rip with his cloak, and when the director yelled "cut," Nelson offered, "I'll do it again if you want, but there's an awful draft up my back."

The wafer-thin plot of *Sweethearts* allowed for gentle spoofing of the MacDonald-Eddy personae. It strove to find new ways of presenting the singing team in logical settings for songs, whether in the show-within-the-show, the recording studio, or elsewhere. Ray Bolger, whose long-legged antics had been deleted from *The Girl of the Golden West*, provided some lively moments in this film. With Miss Mac-Donald he performs "Jeanette and Her Little Wooden Shoe" in which she is garbed in a cute Dutch outfit.

Adrian, whose elaborate creations were the envy of the American housewife, had ample occasion to design a contrasting wardrobe for Jeanette. The film even boasted a fashion-show scene in which she wore nine different creations, ranging from a brown and beige hostess gown to a black-and-white cowboy slacks outfit.

What was most noticeable about the screen team in *Sweethearts* was their togetherness. Never before had they dueted so much on camera. Here they harmonized on "Pretty As a Picture," "Mademoiselle," "I Bring a Breath of Springtime," "Little Grey Home in the West" and the title tune. *Sweethearts* proved to be an outstanding moneymaker in 1938. *New York Times'* critic Bosley Crowther appropriately termed it "a dream of ribbons, tinsel, Technicolor, and sweet, theatrical sentiment." The general public adored it.

With the wide acceptance of this film, M-G-M, in a sudden policy change, reasoned anew that they could make twice as much money if Jeanette and Nelson went their separate professional ways, for a time. Metro starred Nelson in two unmemorable features, the musical *Balalaika* (with Ilona Massey), and *Let Freedom Ring*, the latter a would-be historical pageant.

Meanwhile, Jeanette's screen appearances kept her in the twentieth century and provided her with a new leading man, individualistic Lew Ayres. Robert Z. Leonard was again chosen to direct Jeanette in the project entitled *Broadway Serenade*. It was a standard, if tattered, tale of a married show-business couple. Jeanette is the opera singer who rises in her profession while her temperamental composer-husband is forced to work as a barroom pianist. Later they divorce, but are reunited when his symphonic extravaganza is purchased as a Broadway vehicle for his star-wife.

Lifting the film out of the mundane was the genius of Busby Berkeley. The ex-Warner Bros. choreographer-stager-director was hired on special assignment to bolster the project, to make it something worthy of a Jeanette MacDonald film. As Berkeley recalls it:

> They wanted the thing created in short order because Jeanette had to leave [on concert tour]. I put on my thinking cap and came up with an idea that would tell how the composer was inspired to write the piece after hearing a melody played by a shepherd. I had the art director build me a huge set in varying elevations, all covered with black oilcloth. I wanted a hundred musicians and thirty male singers dressed in black frocks and wearing specially made Benda masks to represent all the great composers. Then there would be twenty female singers dressed in simple flowing black dresses, with Jeanette wearing a beautiful cape and gown. After the composer had heard the shepherd's melody, he sets to work transforming it into a symphony. This gave me a transition —with the completed composition I had my musicians in full dress banked high on the left of the screen with the boy and girl singers in evening suits and gowns on the right of the screen—all of this surrounding a thirty-foot-high pedestal on which Jeanette stood and sang her lyrics. I again insisted on using only one camera but I had it mounted on a large boom with the cameraman and myself on either side, and I made that thing practically float through the air.

The segment was derived from the symphonic composition Herbert Stothart had made from Tchaikovsky's song "None But the Lonely Heart," and it gave *Broadway Serenade* some much-needed importance. (It also won Berkeley an M-G-M contract.)

Lew Ayres has fond recollections of working with Jeanette.

> It was her personal character . . . which impressed me the most. . . . She had more dignity with warmth, exuberance

119

tempered with a sweet, calm control, graciousness unsullied by affectation than any other person I've ever known . . . above it all a most delightfully whimsical sense of humor.

I remember one scene where I was presumably accompanying her singing. The prerecorded playback was necessarily on, as usual, very loud . . . in order to make the task of matching easier. At some point, after many takes, Jeanette happened to catch me making a wry face to someone offstage. Actually, I was jokingly making a reference to the overwhelming volume of her voice on the playback. When I knew she had seen me I only hoped she would understand; explaining would have been too difficult. Nothing was said at the time, but an hour later a package arrived on the set for me containing a carton of anti-noise ear stopples. Accompanying the stopples was a note—a very charming note—saying that this was a service, normally and willingly provided by Miss MacDonald to anyone engaged on her productions. With a serious face I passed them around and about half a dozen of us wore them that day . . . to the merriment of all . . . especially Jeanette.

One person not connected directly with *Broadway Serenade* who had unkind things to say of Jeanette's performance was Grace Moore. In her Columbia film, *One Night of Love,* the musical highlight had been her performance of "Un Bel Di" from *Madame Butterfly,* complete with a Japanese bridge setting. In *Broadway Serenade,* Jeanette also sang "Un Bel Di," on the biggest, highest Japanese bridge imaginable. In a newspaper interview that reeked with acid, Miss Moore alluded to Jeanette's interpretation of Puccini and commented, "The height of the bridge does not determine the quality of the Butterfly."

After completing *Broadway Serenade,* Jeanette's M-G-M contract was due for renegotiation. She had already made plans for an extensive concert engagement and would not postpone it for any discussions. She left the matter in the hands of her lawyers. M-G-M was in a dither, but she was insistent upon returning to the concert stage. One of the compositions she included in her repertory was "Let Me Always Sing," composed by Gene especially for her.

Any doubts of Jeanette's personal popularity were quashed on this

120

crosscountry junket. She had more offers for appearances than she could possibly handle. In fact, she turned down some bids at $25,000 per engagement. When she returned to California she signed the biggest deal of her life at M-G-M, who had been apprised of her tremendous success.

Having settled in again at Twin Gables, Jeanette soon reported to the recording studios for further Victor records. Among the tunes she sang into the microphone were "When I Have Sung My Songs," "Do Not Go, My Love," "Ave Maria," and her very special favorite, "Les Filles de Cadix." With Giuseppe Bamboschek accompanying her on the piano she made a recording of Gene's "Let Me Always Sing," but everyone agreed that it could be done better. On October 5, she returned to the studio and with Gene at the piano she recorded "Let Me Always Sing." This time the magic was there and Victor released the record, somehow forgetting to imprint on the labels of the 78 r.p.m. discs who the famous pianist on the recording was. Gene always claims he never minded; he just wanted the best for his "Bunko."

At this juncture Louis B. Mayer decided it was time to reconsolidate the MacDonald-Eddy screen magic, and teamed them for *New Moon*. Based on Sigmund Romberg's famed operetta which had enthused Broadway in 1928 for 518 performances, the studio had filmed it in 1930 as a vehicle for Lawrence Tibbett and Grace Moore. For the 1940 edition, Metro altered the plot line once again, turning it into a poor rehash of *Naughty Marietta*. It was hoped to duplicate the magnificent success of that earlier MacDonald-Eddy coalition.

If the public could not be given something truly fresh in *New Moon*, the studio certainly replayed the old hit with vigorous, bountiful production values. During the course of the film about a Parisian noblewoman romanced by a pirate, Jeanette wore sixteen different costumes. One particular emerald-green velvet creation weighed eighty-five pounds. Jeanette's portable dressing room, decorated in tones of DuBarry blue and rose, had to be fitted with a double door to allow entrance by the star wearing dresses with skirts more than six feet wide. Even with the doors, Jeanette had to move in and out of her château-on-wheels sideways.

Producer-director Robert Z. Leonard had learned his lesson well about keeping a light air on the set. As Jeanette would recall, "Once he relieved a period of tension by arranging for me to find, to my horror,

121

a strange man asleep on my couch when I went into my dressing room —a man who, on closer inspection, turned out to be a dummy."

The strain of attempting to maintain a freshness about their screen interaction was visible in *New Moon*. Eddy, grown more plump and more wooden, sought to add "spontaneous" touches of witticism to his performance. The effort did not pass muster. Jeanette, the experienced light comedienne, outshone her co-star in the acting department. If Eddy could not be magically transformed into a slick swashbuckler à la Errol Flynn, Jeanette, at least, could provide any quality (except extreme youth) that an Olivia de Havilland-type heroine did on screen.

Occasionally, the screen would come alive with a seemingly spontaneous moment of *joie de vivre*. At one point, late in the story, the couple are in their honeymoon "shack" and Jeanette demands that she be on one side of the bedroom door and Nelson on the other. As she is locking the bedroom door, she accidentally drops the heavy wooden bar on her toes. Eddy rushes to her side.

EDDY: Don't you know I am a specialist?
MACDONALD: A doctor?
EDDY: No . . . a footman.

They had some fine Oscar Hammerstein II-Romberg songs to sing. Eddy was in good voice for "Softly as in a Morning Sunrise" and for the virile "Stout Hearted Men" number with the bondsmen. (It seemed every Eddy-MacDonald operetta ran to formula and the inclusion of a vigorous marching number had become *de rigeur*.) Jeanette offered "I Was a Stranger in Paris" and "Lover Come Back to Me." Together they dueted "Wanting You," a cynical "Our Sincere Appreciation" and a reprise of the captivating "Lover Come Back to Me."

Although *New Moon* was reasonably popular with audiences— there were devout, ever-growing Jeanette MacDonald and Nelson Eddy fan clubs everywhere—many critics found it wanting. Bosley Crowther in the *New York Times* explained:

> Somehow the familiar lilt of the old MacDonald-Eddy extravaganzas is missing from this *New Moon*. Both the principals still give with all the winsome but slightly ponderous charm they possess in the dramatic interludes . . . but it never quite comes alive. . . . With tears welling in our eyes

122

. . . we rather sadly suspect that this sort of sugar-coated musical fiction has seen its better days.

It was true, America was out of its Depression blues and soon would be engulfed in World War II, already rampaging abroad. Times and tastes were changing, but neither the public nor M-G-M, at this juncture, could quite bear to give up on old friends and formats.

While Jeanette embarked on her now annual concert tour and Gene returned to the screen after a year's absence (RKO signed Raymond and cast him in *Cross-Country Romance*), M-G-M tried to do better by its singing love team. After all, it had the sweeping profits of *Gone with the Wind* and other box-office bonanzas like *The Wizard of Oz* and the Mickey Rooney-Judy Garland musical *Babes in Arms* to offset the cost.

Back in 1933 Jeanette had been considered for a filming of Noël Coward's lavender and old spice *Bitter Sweet*, but negotiations fell through and England's Anna Neagle starred in the British picture. Now Metro determined to refilm the property—in color—as the next MacDonald-Eddy venture.

W. S. Van Dyke II, the man who directed the couple's two most financially profitable operettas, *Naughty Marietta* and *Rose-Marie*, was again at the helm. But nothing could offset the revamped, diluted script which destroyed the beauty of Coward's original, charming stage piece.

Bitter Sweet imitated *Maytime* through its initial use of a prologue and an epilogue. Before the film's release in November, 1940, however, the studio eliminated the prologue and epilogue, fearing an unfavorable comparison to the earlier *Maytime*.

As in the earlier film, Jeanette's character (here Sarah Millick) had to age greatly, and this provided a challenge for makeup expert Jack Dawn. He prepared three life masks of Jeanette, and then by experimenting with a rubberlike substance he called "formula six" composed segmental latex alterations for her to apply as she "aged."

If *Bitter Sweet* proved nothing else, it showed (to Jeanette) that redheads could wear red. Once she arrived at the studio in a shade of vermillion called "sunburn." The burn was so severe that a Hungarian costume she was to wear had to be redesigned with a higher neck, and while modeling the outfit on camera, the star had to keep her smiling face in full view of the all-revealing lens.

Demonstrating that the film was almost decadent in its slavishness to production values, a scene featuring a series of peasants had the poor souls, the "glamour peasants," wearing sixty-five yards of material each, covering taffeta petticoats, a total worth of $325 each.

As with most every major studio film of the time, no matter what the quality of the production, the supporting cast could always be counted on for redeeming entertainment values. *Bitter Sweet* was no exception. There was George Sanders as the monocled cad, Veda Ann Borg as the rough-and-ready dupe of the chic set, Felix Bressart and Curt Bois as Eddy's jovial Vienna pals, Diana Lewis as Jeanette's featherbrained London friend, Herman Bing as a bewildered shopkeeper and rotund Greta Meyer as the bubbling beer garden owner.

One could only wonder why Coward's "If Love Were All" had been discarded from the array of songs included in the film. The theme song of the picture is "I'll See You Again," initially sung by Jeanette and Eddy at the London party, then redone at a later audition, and finally at the climax where MacDonald duets with the heavenly spirit of Eddy in yet another rendition of the melody. The couple also jointly sing "Dear Little Café." On her own, Jeanette sings "Love in Any Language," "Ladies of the Town" (with a charming pseudo-Parisian accent), and in her traditional operetta form the "Zigeuner" song from Eddy's posthumously produced stage work. On the other hand, Nelson and chorus provide "Tokay," while singly he croons "The Call of Life"and "If You Could Only Come With Me."

Bitter Sweet was the first financial failure of the MacDonald-Eddy team. The critics pounced on the plot the *New York Sun* termed "as gushing as a schoolgirl's poem." Bosley Crowther, the man from the *New York Times* who mourned the descent of screen operetta, now attacked the genre's premier stars, pronouncing, "Miss MacDonald and Mr. Eddy play it all with such an embarrassing lack of ease—she with self-conscious high-spirit and he with painful pomposity." The *New York Morning Telegraph* asked bluntly, "Isn't it about time that either Mr. Eddy or Miss MacDonald went their separate ways, looking for scripts, instead of just music?"

There were economical factors in addition to *déjà vu* contributing to the poor showing of *Bitter Sweet*. With the war in Europe, eleven countries were closed to English-speaking movies, and Jeanette and Nelson's movies were always extremely popular on the Continent. On

124

the home front, Metro had a new star team that was wooing the customers at the cinemas. Mickey Rooney (number one at the box office) was being profitably paired with Judy Garland and in 1940 under Busby Berkeley's guidance turned out *Strike Up the Band*. And there was the diverting competition of the song-and-dance team (for the first and only time) of Metro's Fred Astaire and Eleanor Powell in *Broadway Melody of 1940*. Veteran Clark Gable, long one of Leo the Lion's biggest customer-drawing stars, found increased favor when he was matched this year with blonde Lana Turner.

Jeanette was now thirty-seven and Nelson was thirty-nine, both a little too old to be toying with the doll-like scripts handed them in the last two years.

With established male idols soon to go off to war, the accent more than ever would be on youth. And, as they say, the camera does not lie, or not usually.

CHAPTER EIGHT

With Jeanette's screen relationship with Nelson Eddy ossifying, everyone ventured, "Why not team Miss MacDonald with her real sweetheart, Gene Raymond?" So they did.

For all their supposed wizardry, studios can be awfully naive. Why in the world would a stale property like *Smilin' Through* be selected as the next project for an actress suffocating from an overdose of sugar laced in ancient material?

Smilin' Through, her only 1941 release, had been filmed twice before, once in 1922 with Norma Talmadge, and again in 1932 with Norma Shearer. Wartime audiences had to be awfully indulgent not to chuckle at the creaking plot, despite the considerable talents of director Frank Borzage and screen writers Donald Ogden Stewart and John Balderstone. Here Jeanette plays an Irish lass whose guardian (Brian Aherne) refuses to allow her to wed her beau (Gene) because the latter's father (Gene again) killed the guardian's wife (Jeanette again) years before.

Although the studio failed to provide solid topical story material, production values were again tops. The wedding gown Jeanette wears in the picture was made of the last seventy-five yards of a priceless imported French lace of crown pattern worn before the French Revolution. It had been brought over by designer Adrian several years before when he journeyed to Paris to buy material for the court scenes of 1938's *Marie Antoinette*. Since the lace was invaluable, the studio made plans to preserve it as an historical artifact, once shooting was completed.

Great care was taken with the construction of an English garden and a flowing brook, as much of the motion picture was shot in these particular settings. For the garden, six hundred shrubs were imported (despite wartime conditions). Some 1,450 feet of grass were woven into the constructed floor of the indoor-outdoor set. Three willow trees and thousands of flowers gave the set a lush, colorful, pastoral quality. (When it was belatedly discovered that Jeanette was allergic to real flowers, artificial ones were substituted.) The trees themselves were replaced several times during the six weeks of filming, in keeping with the time span dictated by the script. The long, sinuous studio brook unwound into a two-hundred-foot stretch, and used 2,000 gallons of water daily.

The brook posed a slight problem for the desired balance of sound. If the noise of the "babbling" brook exceeded a certain decibel, director Borzage signalled the sound man with a white flag, which indicated a lower level be set. Human actors did not always act so efficiently on cue. For example, when the action was set in the abandoned Wayne mansion, thick with cobwebs, soot, dust and grime, allergy-prone Jeanette began sneezing and sneezing—all uncalled for in the script. But at the end of the particular scene in the house, both Jeanette and Gene were to sneeze on cue.

"All right, Jeanette," called director Frank Borzage, "now sneeze when I drop my handkerchief." He gave the cue. Silence. Again the scene was tried—again the cue given—again silence. Finally Jeanette gave up, crossed the room out of camera range. And immediately "kachoo" split the air. "I'm sorry, Frank," she sniffed. "I just can't sneeze on cue."

Among the props brought to *Smilin' Through* was a grandfather clock taken from London in 1932 by M-G-M set decorator Edwin B. Willis. The clock was reportedly 175 years old. The antique desk in Brian Aherne's den was found in a small Irish hamlet. Viennese tapestries and Irish lace decorated the sets, and Italian iron fireplace fixtures were reproduced from six-hundred-year-old models.

Jeanette sang nine solo numbers in *Smilin' Through*, among them the title tune, "Hope and Glory," and "Drink to Me Only."

The film's dialogue, unfortunately, was not exactly in tune with the spirit of Forties' audiences, who were more bent on beating the Axis then sniffling into hankies. (This is not to suggest that *Smilin' Through* did not have its staunch disciples.) For example, near the film's finale, through plot contrivance and the magic of love, the young lovers are reunited.

RAYMOND: Moonyean! . . . . At last you've come to me!

JEANETTE: No. You've come to me. It's been so lonely without you.

RAYMOND: I almost made an awful mess of things. I'm getting very old. And you—you're still young, just as you were. . . .

JEANETTE: Old! John? *You?*

Critics were generally unkind, Bosley Crowther in the *New York Times* being a typically negative pundit. "In brief, the *Smilin' Through* story is pretty mawkish and old hat." One critic was, however, kind to the new screen team of MacDonald and Raymond. "It's their first picture together and Jeanette plays the love scenes so realistically that director Frank Borzage has dubbed himself 'the forgotten man.' "

While Jeanette was performing on the Metro lot with her husband, Nelson Eddy starred with Rise Stevens in *The Chocolate Soldier,* a film turned down by Maurice Chevalier a half dozen years earlier. M-G-M had expressly purchased the rights to *Show Boat, The Vagabond King* and other properties for Jeanette and Nelson, but somehow the time never seemed ripe to produce them, at least with MacDonald and Eddy.

While Jeanette was rehearsing with teacher Grace Newell and then embarking on her next concert tour, Gene was preparing to enter military service. He would enlist in the U.S. Air Force Intelligence Service. After training at Randolph and Kelly Fields in the United States, he would later become Captain Gene Raymond, attached to the 97th Heavy Bombardment Group in England as a B-17 and a B-25 pilot.

Jeanette may have had vanity about her chronological age in her personal life, but she was objective enough to realize that she should no longer be playing coy young things on camera. The problem was she could not convince the Metro authorities of this fact. Their theory was, "If it was good enough in *Naughty Marietta,* it is good enough today."

129

I Married an Angel, released July 9, 1942, was the last film to feature Jeanette and Nelson as a team. In name only, it was the same property that Metro had originally commissioned in 1933 to launch Jeanette's career on the M-G-M lot, but had ultimately rejected as being somewhat immoral. Instead, authors Rodgers and Hart brought their work to Broadway in 1938 where it enjoyed good success. It was generally agreed that the screen version of *I Married an Angel* was uncharacteristically shoddy, and the material itself did not translate to the screen at all well. As for Jeanette and Nelson, they were both now eager to complete their Metro contracts and to leave the lot. They knew when they had been beaten.

The rather fanciful script proposed a series of casting problems. The plot line required twelve extremely beautiful but very tall girls, five midgets, a man with a "cheese" type face, a six-foot-tall man who weighed no more than 125 pounds, a 300-pound woman, and two identical beautiful blondes.

The casting problems having been solved, the studio turned to create its usually impressive production backgrounds (now curtailed because of wartime restrictions). Often the backgrounds were designed to match the costumes. For example, when a Cleopatra-like gold-lace creation was worn, the actress drifted to a set of black-and-gold columns, reminiscent of royal Egypt. Even Nelson Eddy contributed to the look of the film. An amateur sculptor, Eddy made two statues which can be viewed in an early scene in the bank.

Some of Jeanette's most unique costumes were a Zelina skin cape, with a hula skirt of green cellophane, and an angel outfit, composed of a robe, a feathered bodice and a pair of wings she had to strap on with a steel belt.

W. S. Van Dyke II (now a military major) directed the lackluster proceedings, with Bob Wright and Chet Forrest providing additional lyrics to the original score. In this instance, repetition did not make the heart grow fonder as, together or separately, Jeanette and Nelson constantly repeated the title tune. In union they also sang "Spring Is Here" and "I'll Tell Every Man in the Street." Miss MacDonald soloed "Song with the Harps" and Eddy offered "May I Present the Girl." Jeanette had her moments of versatility as she performed the trio from *Faust* and the gypsy song from *Carmen* and executed a Hawaiian hula (a double performed most of the gyrations). But the few bits of real sparkle came from the subordinate cast. Prize buffoon Edward Everett Horton offered a smooth recitative of the "Birthday Song" and expert Binnie Barnes shone with "A Twinkle in Your Eye."

Although Jeanette enthusiastically makes an entrance sliding down a bannister, backed by one hundred harpists, *I Married an Angel* thudded in a manner unknown to the typical celestial being. (The starring couple had previewed the film on "Hollywood Radio Theatre" on June 1, 1942, but it did nothing to whet the appetite of a satiated public.)

I Married an Angel offended a great number of critics. "It's hardly a musical anymore!" carped Herbert Cohn of the *Brooklyn Daily Eagle*. "Between Eddy and MacDonald the middle European fantasy, *I Married an Angel*, becomes a laborious dream indeed, more nightmare than anything else" (Archer Winsten, *New York Post*). "At best Jeanette MacDonald and Nelson Eddy are not exactly a pair of sylphs and no one should willfully embarrass them by asking that they pretend that they are" (Bosley Crowther, *New York Times*).

Jeanette and Nelson were also vastly disappointed in the feature. Eddy provided a useful post mortem for *I Married An Angel:*

> In our films together, Miss MacDonald and I always depicted pure love and we had a lot of trouble with this script because religious groups disapproved of an angel going to bed with a man. Everybody on the lot told us it was either going to be the best picture we ever did, or the worst. It was the worst. It took the studio years to figure out how to present it without offending anybody and then they slashed it to pieces. When we finally finished it, it was a horrible mess.

I Married an Angel finished Nelson Eddy at M-G-M. The next year he would play the romantic lead in Universal's remake of *The Phantom of the Opera* with Claude Rains in the title role. In 1944 he was spotlighted in *Knickerbocker Holiday* with Constance Dowling, and had an off-camera role in the 1946 Walt Disney cartoon feature *Make Mine Music.* In 1947 he would perform with Ilona Massey in

131

Republic's *Northwest Outpost,* a Western which beat two dead horses, the screen operetta and a singer named Eddy. It was his last film.

On the other hand, Jeanette would make one more film under her expiring Metro agreement, the low-budget spy spoof *Cairo.* It was directed by Major W. S. Van Dyke II and would be his next-to-last film assignment. He died on February 5, 1943.

A fair espionage satire, *Cairo* may have been the first Jeanette MacDonald feature to illustrate topical problems, whether on screen or off.

Lena Horne was originally scheduled to play the role of a wise-cracking maid, which was finally essayed by Ethel Waters. Being black, Miss Horne was a difficult property for M-G-M to market in a conventional manner. For the most part, she was sandwiched into special musical sequences of Metro films which could be edited out of prints destined for Southern audiences. She tells the *Cairo* story this way:

> My first screen test, which came after the signing of the contract, was a farce. They were planning a picture co-starring Jeanette MacDonald and Robert Young and were thinking of Eddie Anderson (Rochester) and me to play their servants and, I guess, to have a romance in the film too. It was a good role—the maid was to be just as flippant and fresh as anyone. She was a human being, not a stereotype. They asked Rochester and me to do a test together. They wanted me to match Rochester's color so they kept smearing dark makeup on me. And then they had a problem in lighting and photographing me because, they said, my features were too small. Meantime, poor Rochester had to stand around and wait while they fussed over me. It was embarrassing to me, though he was very pleasant about it. In the end, the test was a disaster. I looked as if I were some white person trying to do a part in blackface. I did not do the picture: Ethel Waters got the part.

Another interesting aspect of *Cairo* was the pre-"New Wave" (but very Bob Hope) references to other films in the script. In one scene, *San Francisco* is mentioned. A clip from *Maytime* is shown, and near the end of *Cairo,* Jeanette and Ethel Waters enter a movie theater and pass by a picture of Nelson Eddy hanging from the wall. In this way, *Cairo* was ahead of its time.

While Jeanette performed some typical singing in "Keep the Light Burning Bright in the Harbor" and "The Waltz Is Over," she did not mind joining in the kidding of her image. At one point in the story, she is requested to sing a high C note, because the vibration will open a secret door panel. She breathes deeply and lets loose an upper register tone, but nothing happens. With a twinkle in her eyes, she informs her comrades that she must admit her tone, of all things, had been off pitch.

Cairo was an anticlimactic swan song for Jeanette, not given much of a sales pitch by the Metro sales force.

But times had changed in the industry and especially at M-G-M. In 1942 not only would Jeanette make her final long-term contract film at the studio, but such perennials as Norma Shearer and Greta Garbo would depart the lot. The next year would find Joan Crawford, once the darling of the studio, transferring to Warner Bros. It was now the age of Judy Garland, Greer Garson, Esther Williams, Lana Turner, Margaret O'Brien and June Allyson.

Any regrets Jeanette had about leaving Mr. Mayer's film factory she kept discreetly to herself. She had bigger plans in the offing.

CHAPTER NINE

The Raymonds were no different from thousands of other couples confronted by Pearl Harbor's tragic chain of events.

When Gene had returned from the President's Birthday Ball in January, 1942, he had announced his application for the Armed Services. When his acceptance from the Air Force had been wired to Twin Gables, Jeanette acted pleased. She knew it was what he wanted. But her true emotion was the anxiety of all those who remain behind while loved ones go off to war.

Of course, the biggest emotional scene was the packing of Gene's bag. Although they had been separated before, when he went East or she gave concerts on tour, this was something quite different. He would not wear his uniform in studio publicity pictures, and she was angered when some persisted in suggesting his enlistment was merely a publicity ruse. Jeanette hostessed a going-away party for Gene, but even then he refused to wear his Air Force uniform in front of a few close friends. He was not interested in sympathy, only in accomplishing the job chosen for him.

Gene's training involved a grueling schedule. Not wanting to leave his wife, Gene brought Jeanette to Arizona with him. He would rise at dawn each morning, and return around six P.M., totally exhausted, but happy he had someone to whom he could come "home."

When they finally parted, Jeanette was brave, comforted by the fact that many had faced her situation before, and would doubtless be confronted with it again. She had some joy in reading the note Gene

135

scribbled on the plane after he left. It concluded, "Thank you, darling, for being you."

She later reflected on her common predicament. "It's as if, standing alone, you feel a hand takes each of yours and suddenly you're not alone but shoulder to shoulder with an army."

Jeanette's life took on a new routine, filled with the verve she expressed when reaching into new territory. Gone were the Sunday morning breakfast treats at the Twin Gables estate with Jeanette presiding over a menu of juice, scrambled eggs with bacon or sausages, waffles, marmalade, maple syrup and coffee. Finished for the duration were Jeanette and Gene's joint trips to Palm Springs to enjoy the warmth of the sun and to exercise on the golf courses. (Jeanette, of course, could continue to sunbathe at her home pool. She swam but hardly ever dived for a sudden rush of water into the sinus area could have produced severe complications.)

But the superstar still pursued her diversified business interests. She owned an apartment building on Alden Drive in Beverly Hills (as well as other California and New York property). Frequently Jeanette could be spotted on early morning walks with her dogs, her hair usually wrapped in a bandanna. Quite often she would stop to talk to workers on the street.

Although Jeanette had commenced her concert career in earnest in 1939, she was now free of her studio obligations and could perform in public more often, a fact she loved. She much preferred the concert stage to, say, radio recording studios and their select audiences. As she explained the dangers of radio studio attendants:

> They're likely to distract the singer and cheat the great listening audience. Particularly in a small audience, the singer cannot avoid noticing when heads are bobbing in approval or disapproval. There's a great temptation to sing to the few in the seen audience instead of singing for the great listening audience which of course one cannot see.

Her concerts were always well planned, as she was extremely concerned with the proper use of makeup, costuming, lighting, etc., and was herself very knowledgeable in those areas.

Many have felt she was even more beautiful in concert than on

136

the screen. Her always expressive face and hands became even more so in person, and her blue-green irises seemed to reflect the depth of her soul. In short, on stage she could radiate the warmth and conviction that was generally blocked out by the one-dimensional nature of the movie screen. Her great performances on the stage betrayed an actress concerned with dramatically interpreting a song as well as projecting its tune with clarion tones. And what songs they were!

For instance, in her concert of February 24, 1941, she sang compositions of Mozart, Schumann, Debussy, Granados, Obredors, Hageman, and Barbour, besides Scottish folk songs and numbers written by Gene Raymond ("Let Me Always Sing," and "Will You?"). Jeanette would gracefully move to the spotlight, frequently wearing a lavender dress with long sleeves which came to points on her petit hands. The dress flowed down in the back with a crisscross effect. At the center of her waist was a corsage of wine and pink flowers.

On that Friday, February 24, for example, the audience insisted on nine encores. She sang, among other selections, "Will You Remember (Sweetheart)," "Italian Street Song," "Indian Love Call," "Ah, Sweet Mystery of Life," and "I'm Not What You Think I Am," the latter a song about a naughty French actress.

She would coordinate any song offered with subtle dramatic movements of the hand or face. This technique was undoubtedly influenced by her years as a movie actress.

A spring tour by Jeanette would follow this typical example:

February 12, El Paso; 15, Dallas, Texas; 17, Shrevesport, Louisiana; 19, Mobile; 21, Birmingham; 23, Montgomery, Alabama; 26, Richmond, Virginia; 28, Washington, D.C.

March 1, Baltimore, Maryland; 4, Harrisburg; 6, Raleigh, North Carolina; 9, Lynchburg, Virginia; 11, Springfield, Massachusetts; 13, Albany, New York; 15, Philadelphia, Pennsylvania; 18, Toledo, Ohio; 20, Springfield, Illinois; 24, Grand Rapids, Michigan; 27, Dayton, Ohio; 29, Chicago, Illinois.

April 1, Milwaukee, Wisconsin; 3, Elmhurst, Illinois; 5, St. Paul, Minnesota; 8, Des Moines, Iowa; 10, Kansas City, Missouri; 12, Wichita, Kansas; 15, Denver, Colorado; 19, San Francisco; 25, Los Angeles.

If newspaper interviews of the day can be believed, Jeanette's favorite preconcert activity, when the situation permitted, was walking

137

through a cemetery. She found it peaceful and not at all morbid. It allowed her to commune with her thoughts and God before undergoing the strenuous performance.

Perhaps the concerts which gave Jeanette the most joy during the war years were the ones she performed for Army Emergency Relief, Inc., as well as the ones for G.I.'s on U.S.O. tours, and at the Hollywood Canteen. She herself was a member of the American Women's Voluntary Service.

One particular concert was as typical as the next of her giving her all for the victory effort. For example, on September 17, 1942, she gave a recital for the Army Emergency Relief, Inc., backed by the 104th Cavalry Regimental Band. Before Jeanette came on stage, the band played several selections. When they turned to "The Star Spangled Banner," Jeanette entered and led the standing audience in song. She was beautifully clothed in a white gown with blue trim around the arms, and on a panel of white net there were blue flowers. She wore a diamond necklace and bracelet (shaped like a clef) and the large diamond ring given her by Gene.

First, she sang Scottish folk songs, then she asked the appreciative audience if they wished to hear "Smilin' Through." They did. After a variety of numbers, she launched into a selection of American songs, two of which were written by Gene. A bit later she sang from the classics, such as "The Waltz Song" from *Romeo et Juliette,* "Sempre Libra" from *La Traviata,* and a group of Debussy numbers.

Next Jeanette, in her most ingratiating manner, requested the audience to purchase as many war defense bonds as they could possibly afford. She joked that although she was Scottish, she would do many encores if the audience would contribute to Army Relief, to the tune of, say, $500. There was no initial response, so she broke the ice by passing the hat around herself, then sang "Indian Love Call." While doing encores, she heard a request from a man in the audience for "One Dozen Roses." She slipped backstage and emerged with a bouquet of red roses presented to her by an admirer before the program. Passing the hat had collected under $200, so Jeanette promised to give the man the roses if he donated the difference. He did! She presented him with the flowers, but had to admit she did not know the song he was requesting.

"Keep the Lights Burning Bright" from *Cairo* was her next tune.

138

WITH NELSON EDDY
IN *NEW MOON* ('40).

WITH ETHEL WATERS
IN *CAIRO* ('42).

IN A POSE FROM
HER 1946
CONCERT TOUR
OF THE BRITISH ISLES.

WITH HUSBAND
GENE RAYMOND.

WITH ANN TODD,
JOSE ITURBI,
JANE POWELL,
AND ELEANOR
DONAHUE IN
*THREE DARING
DAUGHTERS* ('48).

WITH LASSIE IN
*THE SUN COMES
UP* ('49).

WITH HER
HUSBAND AT
"TWIN GABLES."

WITH GENE RAYMOND IN THE STAGE TOUR OF *THE GUARDSMAN* ('51).

AT HER 1957-58 RCA
RECORDING SESSIONS WITH NELSON EDDY.

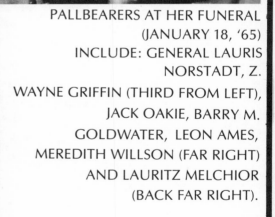

PALLBEARERS AT HER FUNERAL
(JANUARY 18, '65)
INCLUDE: GENERAL LAURIS
NORSTADT, Z.
WAYNE GRIFFIN (THIRD FROM LEFT),
JACK OAKIE, BARRY M.
GOLDWATER, LEON AMES,
MEREDITH WILLSON (FAR RIGHT)
AND LAURITZ MELCHIOR
(BACK FAR RIGHT).

THE SANCTUARY OF
THE HERITAGE.

JEANETTE MACDONALD'S CRYPT.

She sang it twice and received $100 in donations. As the evening was drawing to a close, she had collected about one thousand dollars. Not satisfied, she sent the hat holders out again. Among other selections, she performed "Italian Street Song" for $100. Someone offered $10 for the sheet music of "Indian Love Call," but Jeanette sweetly explained that the orchestra leader, Mr. George Bamboscheck, needed it for eighteen further concerts.

By the end of the night Jeanette had received over $2,500 in donations. She commended the audience, telling them they could "sleep well." She held a cap full of money and pretended it was too heavy as she exited. The concert was a success for Jeanette, the Army Relief, and the audience, who enjoyed every minute of it.

Her ceaseless efforts on behalf of the Army Relief brought in thousands of dollars for the Allied cause, and won her the admiration of hordes of G.I.'s who were thrilled by her natural, unpretentious charm. For a series of twelve concerts, Jeanette turned in $94,681.87 single-handedly for Army Relief. She even sold autographs after those concerts, earning $169.

But one serviceman would not take her autograph—even for free. "Don't you want one, too?" she said to the sailor. "No, thanks," the man replied. "Why not?" asked Jeanette. "You're a married lady," said the sailor gallantly, "and I don't think it would look right for me to be running around with your autograph in my pocket."

Reports of Jeanette's the-show-must-go-on spirit filtered back to Hollywood and to the press. A sergeant at Camp Tyson, Tennessee, reported, "Keep the bells ringing for Jeanette MacDonald. She sang here under the most adverse circumstances (including an unscheduled blackout) and maintained all the charm and poise we like to think our stars possess."

One other young army officer recalled a time Jeanette came to sing at his camp during World War II.

It was early in World War II. Our men were still fighting on Bataan. I was a lieutenant at Fort Mason in San Francisco. There was no USO, nor any program for enter-tainment in those early days. The commanding general had asked if I could get someone to sing the National Anthem at ceremonies for "I Am an American Day." Jeanette said yes

139

without hesitation, but then said if she was coming all that way, couldn't she do something more to help. So on a Sunday afternoon she stood in one of the boxes at the old Dog Racing Track while 20,000 boys headed for the South Pacific sat in the infield. She sang until there weren't any more songs left and still they wanted more. Finally she told them she knew only one more song that was a great favorite of hers, and she started singing the Battle Hymn of the Republic. I will never forget her, nor forget how as she sang, these 20,000 boys came to their feet and finished singing the hymn with her.

The lieutenant, already a well-known actor at the time, became an even better known governor and Presidential candidate, Ronald Reagan.

During this time rumors continually circulated that Jeanette would sign a new movie contract. Both Twentieth Century-Fox (the home of Alice Faye and Betty Grable) and RKO were known to be eager for her cinema services. But she said the only scripts which interested her were ones of a "sophisticated musical" nature.

Jeanette's dream, aside from having Gene home, was to sing opera. To achieve this goal would be a substantiation of her philosophy:

> Life is fluid and keeps moving and motion means change. I know that everything I have now can pass away. . . . Youth passes and the luster of fame dies. There are inevitabilities. You say that I have my voice, too. Yes, but that also can go. It has happened to others. It could happen to me. . . .
>
> I want to be big enough to take the downgrades if they come; to be able to hold the memory of this happiness when, inevitably, some of it must go.

To attempt opera, especially at this mature period of her career, would be risking the scorn of the serious music critics who were never favorably inclined to commercial Hollywood film stars who dared to breach the fold into serious singing.

In early February, 1943, it was announced that her opera debut would be at the Metropolitan Opera that fall, singing *Romeo et Juliette*. But Edward Johnson, general manager of the company, asserted no contract had been signed, or even discussed. It is generally agreed she studied for the role and had plans to tour with the opera before the alleged New York appearance was touted.

It was in late 1942 that Jeanette made the acquaintance of Constance Hope, a dedicated agent for nearly every major singer who appeared at the Metropolitan in those decades. Since Jeanette had ambitions to enter grand opera, it was thought wise to secure an additional agent, who specialized in the field. Helen Ferguson, Jeanette's publicist, agent and friend, remained on the West Coast, while Miss Hope soon became Jeanette's closest friend in Manhattan.

Miss Hope, now Mrs. Constance Berliner, currently lives in New York across the street from Carnegie Hall (in the same building as spry Anita Loos). Her apartment building is moderately old but eminently dignified. It possesses a warm and friendly atmosphere. The warmth extends to the home of Mrs. Berliner and her husband, an eye specialist, and of course, to the woman herself.

One recent, cold morning, she fondly recalled how she came to meet the famous Jeanette MacDonald.

> She was beginning to have a desire to make a mark in serious music, not only in pictures. And she was sent to me by her publicity agent, as a specialist in this field, which I was.
>
> I went to meet her in Baltimore. . . . I had no idea what she was like, and she had no idea what I was like. She came in and I expected the grande dame and she was the grande dame. And she looked beautiful. She had such coloring. . . . She was very pleasant . . . and I was a little impressed, because I didn't have much to do with movie people. . . . We talked. I liked her and she liked me. She wasn't putting on airs.
>
> Her husband was in the army at that time. And she was more alone than normally, and less social naturally because so many of their friends were in the army. When she came to New York, we became even closer. I just worked for her, and she was telling me what her plans were going to be. She was going to do an opera, and that was why I developed into the picture. So, I began to give her advice. . . .
>
> She was going to do *Romeo and Juliet.* I knew the whole

cast. She was engaged by somebody who had engaged the whole cast, and most of them were my clients.

Miss Hope advised Jeanette to attend a ballet version of Shakespeare's tragedy being performed at the time by Markova (another of her clients). Jeanette's new agent believed the ballerina's interpretation of Juliet as "feminine, helpless" was the correct approach to the role. Always wanting to learn, Jeanette went to the ballet and thanked Miss Hope for good advice.

When Jeanette did make her opera debut in *Romeo et Juliette,* co-starred with bass Ezio Pinza, on May 8, 1943, in Montreal, she did so under the worst of circumstances. In the first place, most opera singers will try out a new role in the hinterlands, away from well-meaning friends and carping critics. By the time they face a sophisticated audience, the part will have been honed to their best efforts. But Montreal was a very cosmopolitan city and its citizens very knowing.

Then, too, in Montreal Jeanette contracted a cold. Thus she had to go onstage virtually "auditioning" a new part and performing it in front of a major audience while ill. If the star was suffering from stage fright, it was not apparent. She whisked across the proscenium wearing soft little blue moccasins (blocked from view by the long skirts on her gowns) and sang to critical approval. Her diligence had paid off once again, as she had been coached in the part by the Metropolitan Opera's French bass Léon Rothier. She was also surrounded by experts in the lavish production. Besides Pinza as Friar Laurence, there was Armand Tokatyan as Romeo, and in the pit was noted conductor Wilfred Pelletier.

Thomas Archer, writing of Jeanette's performance in Gounod's opera, at His Majesty's Theatre reported, "It may be said at once, it was in more ways than one an auspicious debut, a triumph for Miss MacDonald and an honor to Montreal. The singer . . . undertook the role of Juliet with a determination and a vocal ability that called for more and more admiration as the evening's proceedings went on."

Conductor Pelletier would later add, "She was a beautiful Juliet, poetic in the balcony scene and passionate in the last two scenes. . . . Her success as an operatic singer was genuine, and as a colleague she was admired and beloved by her companions, the orchestra and the chorus."

After her tour of Canada and the United States in this opera, Jeanette returned to her concertizing, to her war work, and to enjoying the short leaves afforded to Gene. One of her unique contributions to the U.S.O. effort was the "date-leave" plan. The way it went was that every other Sunday, she and Gene (when he was there) would have open house at Twin Gables for ten soldiers and sailors and ten young women. The guests were invited to swim in the stars' pool, to enjoy a hamburger barbeque, and then to dance or play cards and games. Only soft drinks were served at these date-leaves.

Over the years, it had often been suggested that Jeanette's voice, a light lyric soprano, was simply too thin to be taken seriously (outside of movie musicals). It was Constance Hope who thus suggested a union between Jeanette and Lotte Lehmann, the latter a client and personal friend of the influential agent.

Miss Hope remembers:

> I said to her, 'you know Jeanette, you've learned so much about the serious end of music, but you can afford it, and it's possible for you. I want you to put the cherry on the sundae, I want you to be even better than you are. I'd like you to go to Lotte Lehmann, who to me is the greatest opera singer that I have ever seen. . . . Because she combined a beautiful voice, not a great voice, but a beautiful voice, with a quality of communication so that you lived everything with her, and no other opera singer does that. . . . She was like Beverly Sills is today. . . . you followed her and the character came alive, and she was fantastic.

With such a recommendation, Jeanette wasted no time in journeying to Santa Barbara, California, to study with Madame Lehmann. Speaking about Jeanette's experience with Lehmann, Constance Hope in 1975 remarked:

> [Jeanette] called me up that day [after her session with Lehmann]. She wasn't a quick caller-upper. . . . [Jeanette] was

a writer, she didn't spend money. She was not extravagant; she was not small, but she was *not* extravagant.

She called me up and said, "Constance, I wondered what it was that made you say that I should go to Lehmann. But I went to Lehmann, and I can only tell you that an hour with her on a role is as if the room is dark, and you open the windows and sunshine flies in."

Studying with Lotte Lehmann must have aided the naturally dramatic quality Jeanette intoned in every song. She rehearsed thrice weekly with Miss Lehmann, an hour per session. Jeanette's immediate goal was to add the role of Marguerite from *Faust* to her repertory.

When queried some three decades later about her famous pupil, the still active and still quite abrupt Miss Lehmann wrote me, "She had talent, but it was a little too late for her to pursue a career as an opera singer. . . . She responded well and was an excellent performer."

On another occasion, Miss Lehmann was more expansive.

When Jeanette MacDonald approached me for some coaching lessons I was really curious how a glamorous movie star, certainly spoiled by the adoration of a limitless world, would be able to devote herself to another, a higher, level of art. I had the surprise of my life: There couldn't have been a more diligent, a more serious, a more pliable person than Jeanette. The lessons, which I started with a kind of suspicious curiosity, turned out to be sheer delight for me.

She studied Marguerite with me—and Lieder. These were the ones which astounded me most. I am quite sure that Jeanette would have developed into a serious and successful Lieder singer if time would have allowed it.

But alas, movie contracts had to be fulfilled—and perhaps it was right so: we have now simply more of her exquisite records—songs which nobody nowadays can sing as Jeanette.

On Friday night, July 14, 1944, Jeanette got more of a punch out of her rehearsal session than she had anticipated. As was her custom, she frequently stayed over at the El Encanto Hotel in Santa Barbara

144

after her lesson with Miss Lehmann. That night she had just got to bed, when she heard a door slam in her cottage. She arose to investigate. Suddenly someone grabbed the star and attempted to wrap a blanket about her head. Jeanette struggled, kicked and screamed. At that moment, her assailant gave her a stiff punch in the eye. In the course of the melee, he scratched her face. She managed to flash on a light as he fled. The prowler escaped (having stolen nothing), leaving Jeanette with a black and swollen eye and scratches and cuts on her face.

But the bruises were worth it when she appeared in Chicago that November, alternating performances of *Romeo et Juliette* with *Faust*. In the latter opera, Ezio Pinza played Mephistopheles and tenor Raoul Jobin was Faust. The engagement had been sold out for weeks. On opening night she had eight curtain calls. Of course, rehearsing the two diverse roles was tough, and Jeanette would later recall the ordeal as "the grimmest experience of my life."

Unquestionably, Jeanette was ever on the alert during her role playing. In one scene during an actual performance, a knife was left on stage when it should have been out of sight. Jeanette quickly got rid of it, and at least one reviewer noted her quick thinking and remarked on her "presence of mind" which was commendable for a "debut."

Tough-to-please Chicago critic Claudia Cassidy reported of Miss MacDonald's Marguerite that it was "a stage-wise performance as French as Yvonne Gall's, beautifully sung with purity of line and tone, a good trill, and a Gallic inflection that understood the phrasing." As for her critique of Juliet, Miss Cassidy noted that Jeanette "is breathtakingly beautiful to the eye and dulcet to the ear." (A year later Jeanette would again sing *Faust* in Chicago, this time with Nino Martini and Nicola Moscona as her co-stars. Miss Cassidy, now an acknowledged MacDonald booster, wrote, "a singing actress of such beauty you felt if Faust must sell his soul to the devil, at least this time he got his money's worth.")

But the most important critic for Jeanette at any of her performances was the audience. She always insisted, "If it wasn't for my fans, I wouldn't be where I am today." Perhaps the most eloquent, heartfelt tribute to Jeanette came from one of her thousands of avid admirers. Sometime after the Montreal and Chicago performances, the fan wrote:

145

I can remember so happily too the trip I made to Montreal for your world debut in the opera *Romeo and Juliet.* I was at two performances right in the first row thanks to someone's kindness. The second evening one of the violinists spotted me, and remembered me from the previous evening —he came over and spoke to me, and told me that all the members of the orchestra thought you were one of the most gracious singers they had ever met—also commented on your beautiful French. Not so long after that, I attended the performance in Chicago—and there I met your mother. She was so grand to me. When I moved to California she invited me several times. She was kind and a wonderful woman and you are so very like her.

Jeanette's fans and her business agents had been clamoring to see her on the screen again. After many picture deals fell through, including a version of Frances Parkinson Keyes' novel *Crescent Carnival,* and *The Emissary from Brazil,* or *East Wind,* each to co-star her with Nelson Eddy, Jeanette agreed to appear in an all-star movie revue at Universal called *Follow the Boys.* Filmed to entertain the troops (and make use of the studio's contract roster), the potpourri picture featured, among others, Marlene Dietrich, Orson Welles, the Andrews Sisters, Sophie Tucker, W. C. Fields and George Raft. Jeanette sang two songs in the movie, one the popular "Beyond the Blue Horizon." Universal publicity men advised and assured the public that Jeanette would delete "rising sun" from the lyric and would sing it as follows; "Beyond the blue horizon lies the shining sun." Anything to help the anti-Tokyo war effort!

Perhaps the zenith of her professional success during the war years was her concertizing at the Hollywood Bowl in August, 1945. In those days, before acoustical amplification was a requisite for performers to be heard, Jeanette filled the Bowl with a record twenty thousand attendees. After singing encore after encore to the enthusiastic audience, she concluded with songs chosen by the audience—tunes from her pictures. Following this triumph, she and Major Gene Raymond hosted a reception. Among the illustrious guests were Governor and Mrs. Earl Warren, Irene Dunne, Patricia Morison, General and Mrs. Ralph Cousins, Atwater Kent and, from M-G-M, Louis B. Mayer and

Eddie Mannix. Standing in the receiving line with Jeanette was her singing teacher of many years, Grace Adele Newell.

After over twenty-five years in show business, Jeanette was still at her peak.

CHAPTER TEN

In the post-war years of the mid-Forties, tastes and attitudes changed. But one opinion that persisted (and still does) is that Jeanette was too prim for comfort. Yet those who knew Jeanette best could attest she was not a prude.

One little-known verified episode illustrates the point nicely. Jeanette and Gene Raymond were attending a special showing of *Paris-Underground*, the 1945 spy melodrama produced by and starring chic Constance Bennett. At the party following the screening, Jeanette was in a devilish mood. She removed lemon peel from several glasses about her and arranged them on a plate to resemble a breast, complete with nipple. She then summoned a waiter and gave it to him to take to Miss Bennett with the message, "Tell Constance I think she can use this."

Constance looked over at her with a slight frown, and then coyly stuck out her tongue at her. Jeanette giggled and Gene scolded her. This was the other side of Miss MacDonald.

A short time before World War II concluded, Gene completed his tour of duty with the Air Force. (He would later have the rank of colonel and be in the reserve unit, devoting at least two weeks of training per year to the service.) Constance Hope was with Jeanette in New York, and both awaited Raymond's arrival. Miss Hope recollects:

> Finally he was going to be released. She and I were together, all that day, waiting for the word that he was back in New York. I never saw any bride more excited about it than she was. And she had everything prepared. . . . She didn't even want to go out of the house. She was afraid she'd miss the call. . . . There was that kind of a close relationship.

With Gene home, Jeanette continued her career with more enthusiasm than ever. There were several radio reunions with Nelson Eddy in rehashes of their past film successes. Ernst Lubitsch wanted to do a picture with Jeanette, but their timetables never worked out properly. Entrepreneur Mike Todd almost had her signed for a Broadway production, but she kept putting it off as she preferred doing opera or concert work or entertaining servicemen.

From June 30 to July 21, 1946, Jeanette gave seven concerts in Great Britain. She traveled from the Albert Hall in London to the Town Hall in Birmingham on July 3, to Davis Theatre in Croydon on July 7, to Fisher Hall in Edinburgh on July 10, to Theatre Royal in Dublin on July 13, to Philharmonic Hall in Liverpool on July 16, and finally to the New Opera House in Blackpool. (All the proceeds from the Albert Hall concert were donated to the St. Dunstan's Home for the Blind, as she had been so impressed by the organization when she visited the institution.)

Typically, Jeanette was a hit with the majority of critics and fans. The *London Daily Telegraph* reported, "Jeanette MacDonald, better known in this country as a film singer, gave a recital at the Albert Hall last night. She uses her clear and buoyant soprano voice with the skill of wide experience and her platform manner is gracious and effective. Her enunciation was good and phrased with assurance." The critic in that city's *Daily Express* noted rather wittily, "The problem of the Albert Hall's bad acoustics was solved last night by film prima donna Jeanette MacDonald with 24 songs from opera, ballads and from screen material-musicals. Recipe: 1. Fill the hall (the largest audience this year). 2. Sing (her softest notes were heard in the top balcony). 3. Enunciate (every word was clear)."

150

After one concert, Jeanette was besieged to make a speech. A bit later so many autograph hunters filled the streets that a monumental traffic jam ensued.

While Jeanette was in Scotland on this tour, she tried to trace the lineage of her grandmother, Jeanette Johnston, who had left Balfron around 1850 at age twenty-five and had gone to America and married a MacDonald. The investigation proved fruitless.

When Jeanette returned to America, there was much talk of another film. Louis B. Mayer owned the rights to *Blossom Time* and vaguely talked of starring Jeanette in it. Producer Marcel Hellman of London came over to Hollywood to confer with her about an unrealized basically nonmusical film, which would have allowed Jeanette to sing a few songs. In fact, while Jeanette was busy concertizing in Europe, she had relinquished a role at M-G-M that had been designed for her, a key part in *Holiday in Mexico*. The Technicolor feature starred Jane Powell as the musically inclined daughter of ambassador Walter Pidgeon. Jeanette was to have played the woman in Pidgeon's life. When she refused to alter her previously arranged tour, Ilona Massey was substituted. Jeanette promised producer Joe Pasternak that she would make other films for him at M-G-M.

Meanwhile, Jeanette was enjoying domesticity, settling back into Twin Gables with Gene and their assorted dogs (Stormy Weather, Tray and Nick). And when she was not on a rigorous concert schedule, she could relax. Sleep came more easily for her and she could eat a more balanced diet. (On tours she always ate yogurt and fruit before her concerts as she could not digest any other food due to nervousness.)

The year 1947 brought two deaths which affected Jeanette greatly. Two of her great supporters passed away. Ernst Lubitsch died (thus ending hopes of his filming *Der Rosenkavalier* with her as Marschallin) and on May 17 her mother expired.

On an uplifting note, Jeanette went to Mexico City in late October, 1947, to perform three radio broadcasts. She had to fly (flying made her nervous), but Gene was at her side. Although the plane reached the airport two hours late, there were thousands of people awaiting her arrival. She felt quite ill, and really wanted to "run to the room," but this was impossible.

The broadcasts went well, and afterward Jeanette and Gene vacationed in Cuerna Vaca for a few days, "basking the sun." But she could not forget her mother's death. As she wrote a friend, "We plan on having a very quiet Christmas this year and needless to say we will miss mother very much. She always had such fun each year, opening her gifts, and you could just enjoy yourself watching her laugh at all our silly jokes."

Also in 1947, Jeanette announced "I'm through playing Valentine parts." She was persuaded by Metro's Joe Pasternak to accept a co-starring role in a vehicle entitled *The Birds and the Bees.* The title was eventually changed to *Three Daring Daughters*, a name tag which better indicated the nature of the plot. Jeanette plays Louise Rayton Morgan, a widow with three daughters, Jane Powell, Elinor Donahue, and Ann Todd, who try to prevent her marriage to concert pianist Jose Iturbi (played by Mr. Iturbi).

Despite the changes in the star roster and of the executive staff, Jeanette was pleased to be in front of the Metro color cameras again.

It's good to be back! Although it has been five years since my last picture, it seems only a few weeks. Having the same crew, wardrobe girl, and press representative with whom I worked before has helped me to span those years. But I wouldn't take anything for the opportunity I have had to devote to my music, meet the public, and realize a life-long ambition—opera.

The cast, director (Fred M. Wilcox) and crew of *Three Daring Daughters* apparently got along quite well during the seventy-eight days of production. Jeanette particularly liked one of her screen daughters, twelve-year-old Elinor Donahue (who later gained fame as part of the "Father Knows Best" TV family).

Recently, amid the jungle of dishes and glasses in a crowded Los Angeles restaurant, Miss Donahue thought back nearly thirty years, recalling Jeanette.

She was a beautiful, beautiful lady. My memory of her is as you think of a very rich and beautiful aunt that you don't see very often. She was, I think, a shy woman. She didn't sit around the set and mingle with people, for instance. When she finished her shot she'd go back into her dressing room.

152

So she was remote in that respect, but not cold. She was a very warm person.

My memory also is that she adored animals. . . . She had planned a big surprise for my Christmas present, the year that we were doing the movie. And she kept building it up, as this fabulous surprise, [saying] "I can't wait to give it to you!" I was just so excited I couldn't stand it. So the day before the Christmas break, the hairdresser gave me a little tom cat, and I named it after the assistant director . . . and I ran up to Miss MacDonald and said, "Look, look what she gave me for Christmas!"

Her face fell, and she said, "Oh that's lovely dear," and turned and walked away. I thought that was funny, because up to that point she'd been so sweet with me and so warm and she just couldn't wait for Christmas to come. And she was very cold and looked angry. And I went to my mother, and said, "Mother I don't know what I did. I showed Miss MacDonald my kitty, and she got angry."

It turned out that Jeanette had purchased a lovely white angora cat for Elinor and had been keeping it at home until it was time to pass on the Christmas gift.

On the set of *Three Daring Daughters,* Jeanette was more pleased when discussing the wedding ring Gene had given her.

Did you ever hear of a slip cover for a wedding ring? That's exactly what I have, and wear. Somehow I always felt your wedding ring was one ring you never wanted to part with for even a minute. So I solved the problem this way.

In pictures where I play a "single" role, a ring is designed especially to fit over it, and I have a gold "slipcover" to wear over it when my jewelry is gold. There's something else about my ring. I vowed when Gene put it on my finger that I'd never take it off. I've never seen the message engraved inside. Gene has told it to me and you may be sure I know every precious word by heart, but I've never read it myself.

Jeanette, who always wore wigs in her movies, wore ten new hair styles in the film which publicists claimed featured the three "B's": Bach, Beethoven and Boogie! She did not much care for the coiffures, which featured the "Renoir look," or soft curves, waves, and simple lines. Years later Gene Raymond revealed she was forced to wear those particular hair styles because her regular look made her seem too young to be romanced by co-player Iturbi, a man in his fifties.

Her wardrobe, designed by Irene, consisted of a sophisticated bright orange jersey, with a matching stole; a sheer crepe gown of aqua blue; a cocoa lace gown (hand-made lace, of course); and a black chiffon crepe formal, trimmed in gold beads.

Critics passed off *Three Daring Daughters,* which debuted in February, 1948, as a pleasant trifle. There were kind words for Jeanette's vocalizing, as contrasted with the cute soprano singing of Miss Powell, and for Mr. Iturbi's piano virtuosity (ranging from "Liebestraum" to the "Dickey Bird Song"), but not for the plot. The *New York Times* labeled it a "silly little tale" in which Miss MacDonald weds Iturbi. As a postscript the reviewer added, "Despite a build-up of curiosity, Miss MacDonald's first [screen] husband is never revealed. We still want to know who he was. Nelson Eddy, perhaps?" *Time* magazine noted the characters had a "fairly stupid" aura about them.

What the critics did not seem to note, however, was Metro's attempt to make Jeanette's screen persona seem more average, less lofty.

As Elinor Donahue remembers:

> During the movie they decided to . . . humanize her a little bit, so she didn't seem so grand . . . kind of really get some gutsy stuff. So they wanted her to sing "You Made Me Love You," and she didn't want to sing it. . . . But being the lady that she was, she went along with it.
>
> The day that they were filming it, I was on the set going to school. I came out to listen, and I was very puzzled by the singing of it. As only a child would do, I had the temerity to go over to her and say, "You know, you're not singing that right. It's 'Gimme, gimme, Gimme what I cry for. . . .'"
>
> And she said, "No dear. That's the way Mr. Jolson sings it—not the way I sing it."

Those who knew Jeanette well realized that she would not be concerned by the middling reviews for *Three Daring Daughters*. She had learned from friend Helen Traubel that it was wise not to pay much attention to critics, although Jeanette would admit that it was very hard "not to be curious over what someone thinks of your efforts."

On March 30, 1948, Jeanette more than made up for the tepid reviews of her latest film with her concert at Los Angeles' Philharmonic Auditorium. According to Albert Goldberg of the *Los Angeles Times:*

> Radiant and glowing, she stepped onto the stage of Philharmonic Auditorium last night to be greeted rapturously by an audience that filled the place to the rafters and that seemed to be equally compounded of movie celebrities and autograph hunters.
>
> Her vocal resources, judged by concert standards, are limited, but she has studiously and sincerely developed them not only to a point of respectability, but to a general degree of adequacy and versatility.

While Jeanette was busy with concerts, films and recording obligations, Gene had returned to the straw-hat circuit (in 1946) after an absence of eighteen years. His co-star was Gertrude Lawrence and the play was *The Man in Possession.* His movie comeback was RKO's *The Locket*, in 1946, with Laraine Day and Robert Mitchum. Then in 1948 he switched to portraying rough guys on camera in *Assigned to Danger* and *Sofia.* That same year he directed and starred in *Million Dollar Weekend* for a low-budget studio, Eagle-Lion. None of the pictures did much for his career.

On the other hand, Jeanette enjoyed her recent film-making venture (and the salary it paid). She was pleased that the executives and talent at Metro treated her "as if she had never been away." Thus she readily consented to return to the Culver City spread for *The Sun Comes Up*, a color film released early in 1949. Her co-star was none other than Lassie! Being allergic to dogs, she had to undergo special allergy treatment during the making of the film.

The picture craftily revolves around an opera singer, Helen Winter (Jeanette), a woman embittered because of her son's tragic death

155

in a car accident. Eventually she is brought back to caring by another youngster, Jerry (Claude Jarman, Jr., of "The Yearling" fame), and a writer, Tom Chandler (Lloyd Nolan). Interwoven into the plot were lots of vocalizing and the antics of that smart canine Lassie, playing her dead son's beloved pet.

The Sun Comes Up was shot largely on location 375 miles from Hollywood in the Santa Cruz mountains. Transportation vehicles included two trains, seven passenger limousines and one bus. Thirteen local children were recruited to portray Jarman's friends.

While *The Sun Comes Up* never achieves greatness as a bit of Americana and certainly contains no gems of impressive dramatics, it does present Jeanette closer to her real self than any of her other M-G-M films. The true person and not just the prima donna of operetta shines through.

At one point in the story she sings "Songs My Mother Taught Me" to Jerry, the boy she tries so hard not to like (because of the death of her own son). One could almost see the sad memories from Jeanette's own life filling her eyes, as she so poignantly tries to finish the song which ends on a broken little note. It showed how underrated Jeanette's acting ability had always been.

At another juncture in *The Sun Comes Up,* Jeanette's character says, "I'll be all right—once I'm on the stage . . . I'm a professional. . . . It's a nice business." It was so like the real-life Miss MacDonald, as was everything else about the singer in the picture. Here she did not assume a role, she was just being Jeanette, with those special little hand movements and voice inflections.

A great emphasis in the Richard Thorpe-directed feature is placed on Jeanette's attachment to children. It reintroduced the recurring speculation why the Raymonds had never had any of their own. On one occasion, the private-life Jeanette reflected, "No, we were not privileged to have any. That has been the only void in our marriage." For those who knew the Raymonds intimately, the consensus was that not only was the couple collectively and individually too busy to give a child proper care and attention, but Gene never much liked youngsters. "I'm not the child-loving type of person," he once admitted.

Despite Jeanette's and Lassie's presence, *The Sun Comes Up* was received with benign apathy. The *New York Times* dismissed it as "a

156

wholesome, inoffensive, sometimes banal and always standard entertainment."

After so many years of stardom, Jeanette deserved better than
this.

CHAPTER ELEVEN

> Deep down inside me I crave service and attention and
> I loath responsibilities and being "dependable" and there are
> lots of times when I don't feel like being pleasant, and I'd
> rather say "the devil with it" and kick my heels in the air and
> go off on a tangent.
>   But why don't I . . . why haven't I? Because I've always
> made a point of controlling myself, because I always thought
> it was the thing to do.

So spoke Jeanette MacDonald, but she continued on into the
Fifties in the only way of life she had ever really known, show business.
Her television debut occurred on November 11, 1950, on NBC's
"Voice of Firestone," which simulcast a program on both radio and
television. Many video appearances would follow during the decade,
often with Jeanette as a guest artist, but sometimes as a dramatic
performer.

As usual, her concerts were widely lauded by fans and respectfully
critiqued by the press. The fact that she occasionally mispronounced
the name of a composer (for example, enunciating Delibes as "De-
Liebes" and not "Duh-leeb") or confused one songwriter for another
(Johann Strauss for Richard Strauss) was easily forgivable. Her diction
in singing was above reproach. Often not enough credit was given to
the conductor by the audience. For instance at her January, 1949,

concert with the San Francisco Symphony, conductor Pierre Monteaux wisely dampened the orchestra down to double pianissimo at climaxes of "Un Bel Di" so she could be heard. A less knowledgeable conductor could have destroyed her by leading the aria the way it normally would be played.

By the Fifties, Jeanette's enduring fan clubs were also gaining something of a special reputation for their loyalty. For instance, the *Springfield* (Massachusetts) *Union* reported on May 8, 1950:

> Ordinarily, a fan club rates about a paragraph. But not this one.
>
> Tonight when Miss MacDonald appears in the auditorium under the sponsorship of the Business and Professional Women's Club, 24 loyal—and that's the word—members of the club will be in the audience. It doesn't matter that they've heard her in Portland and Worcester during her concert tour. They don't mind saving for a year, as one of them explained in Hotel Kimball yesterday afternoon, because they feel it's worth it to hear her and, when the occasion arises, chat with her for a few minutes.

Understanding and appreciating her fans' devotion, Jeanette felt badly that they traveled about the country to hear her perform a very set series of songs at every concert, and wear a particular line of gowns. "I feel a little guilty. I really ought to throw in a couple of different numbers and wear a different gown. They've heard the same program throughout New England."

The mention of "gown" sparked Jeanette to remember an incident onstage when she almost lost her professional chastity. One evening she was in the midst of a saucy little comedy song when her left shoulder strap gave way at her wide gestures. As the strap snapped Jeanette quickly caught the loose end and finished the song. "That won't happen again," she said happily, "for the maid has reinforced it. But good."

One summer night (July 27, 1950) a Jeanette MacDonald appearance brought approximately 17,000 persons to an outdoor theater in Fairmount Park in Philadelphia. The night was blessed with a soupçon of cool air, and the acoustics were sufficiently balanced to permit

Jeanette's voice to bound all over the park. The Robin Hood Dell Orchestra was conducted by Vladimir Golschmann, and the musicians ably backed Jeanette's many classic and popular numbers. She wore a sparkling gray evening gown with low-cut shoulders, the effects of which caused many listeners to wonder aloud whether she was perhaps only in her thirties, and not really closer to fifty years of age. When the first half of the performance concluded, she was induced out for five curtain calls.

Another time in Lafayette, Louisiana, at the Blackham Coliseum, Jeanette was in a particularly pixieish mood. At one point, a woman stood up from her seat and snapped a photo of Jeanette while the star was singing. The flashbulb drew Jeanette's attention, and she graciously put on an especially bewitching look for the shutterbug. That evening she wore another strapless gown, this time of orchid chiffon, with a chiffon stole angling about her shoulders. Necklace and earrings of rhinestone set off the outfit.

With both Raymonds so fond of stage work, it was only natural for them to select a vehicle in which they might tour jointly. They decided upon *The Guardsman*, which had been such a hit for Alfred Lunt and Lynn Fontanne in the Twenties (and which was the basis for their only film—at M-G-M in 1931). The Raymonds decided to tour in the show and after fifteen weeks to bring the project to Broadway.

The play was readapted to suit the Raymonds' talents, switching Jeanette's character to that of a singer. It allowed her to perform a mini-concert within the comedy. Among the numbers to be sung were a version of "Clair de Lune" with lyrics by Gene. One of the gimmicks in the tour was that Jeanette would substitute songs at will in the mini-concert, depending on the wishes of fans who had written in advance to her. The show featured Herbert Berghoff in a supporting role.

There was much turmoil during the road tour, as conflicts arose between the Raymonds and the producers. According to Gene the scenery was second-rate and the management of the play "desultory." Jeanette complained she had to "furnish my own chinchilla, jewels, oil paintings and hairdo items."

But there were some joyous moments on the trek. During one performance, Gene couldn't locate the false nose he wore for the disguise scene, and he scurried about backstage trying to locate it, while

161

Jeanette was forced to ad-lib and carry on the sequence solo until he made a delayed entrance. On another occasion, the couple, puzzled by the failure of a surefire line to get a laugh, determined to call the Lunts (then on Broadway) to learn how they had handled it twenty-five years earlier. They finally located the famed stage couple at the race track and Alfred Lunt offered some side-seat direction for Gene.

In August, 1951, the Raymonds made an appearance on Ed Sullivan's "Toast of the Town" TV variety program promoting *The Guardsman.* Unfortunately, continued disputes with the producers ended their dream of playing to a New York audience again. By the holidays that year they were back in California, attending small parties with such close friends as the Nelson Eddys and the Cornwall Jacksons (Gail Patrick). Often at these get-togethers Jeanette and Nelson would sing duets together "for old times' sake."

When asked if she would return to films, Jeanette said only if the proper vehicle should be found. At various times she would announce that she planned to produce her own films and that she would not necessarily be the star of the vehicle. A good story and fine entertainment were all that mattered to her. As for returning to M-G-M, she had lost interest in the studio now that Dore Schary was in charge of production. (Her antagonistic sponsor, Louis B. Mayer, would be ousted from the studio in the early Fifties.) Another secret reason for Jeanette's decision to lessen her pace (if that was possible) was her physician's growing concern about her physical condition. It would soon be diagnosed that she had a bad heart; nothing serious, if she did not overtax herself.

Oddly enough, Jeanette was invited to attend a reunion at West Philadelphia High School in 1952. Although she never graduated from the school, on March 29 she was reunited with a group of alumnae. Among the other distinguished graduates, there was Betty Garde, of the original cast of *Oklahoma!* The picture of the happy group taken in the Mirror Room of the Warwick Hotel in Philadelphia shows a group of smiling, middle-aged women.

162

Jeanette's former classmates, including Rose Landesberg Devon, were always impressed that Jeanette had not gone Hollywood. Says Mrs. Devon:

> There was never any sense of anything withheld. She was always cheerfully candid about herself and grew older (or more mature) as frankly and as openly as anyone in the theater or public life. . . .
>
> As much as anyone can leave a scene and be a part of it, Jeanette did. . . . Haughtiness was not in her. We loved her.

When the girls got together to reminisce, they joked about the time when Jeanette was just starting her career, and Rose and some others took her out for a late snack. Jeanette ordered oyster stew and asked the waiter to "take out the oysters, please." (Rose has a photograph of Jeanette autographed, "Yours for oysterless stews.")

Another reunion came as more of a surprise to Jeanette. On Wednesday, November 12, 1952, her friend Helen Ferguson persuaded her to drop by the El Capitan Theatre in Hollywood to present an award. It all sounded a bit vague, but Jeanette agreed. As she drove into the adjacent parking lot, an attendant advised her, "Park your car next to Nelson Eddy's." Jeanette thought nothing of it.

Then events began crowding on one another and almost before she realized it, Jeanette was the subject of Ralph Edwards' TV show, "This Is Your Life." For the woman who once dreamed of buying a limousine and a pink bed for Mother, the reconstruction of her event-jammed life was breathtaking. Jeanette had thought Gene was in New York performing in a TV show, but he soon walked out onto the stage to join her sisters Elsie and Marie Blake and Nelson Eddy and other people from her past.

Jeanette had another reason to be joyous that November. She and Gene had participated in the "I Like Ike" movement. Being staunch Republicans, they were happy to campaign for Eisenhower. (Ike and Mamie became devoted friends of Jeanette's and Gene's and regretted that the General's extreme popularity prevented him from attending her concerts—he drew too much of a crowd and the security men forbade it.) That fall, the Raymonds, along with George Murphy, Irene

163

Dunne, John Wayne and Ward Bond, had promoted the Eisenhower-Richard Nixon ticket in Texas. As celebrants in the Eisenhower Presidential Victory, the Raymonds would later attend the Inaugural Ball.

When not concertizing, Jeanette was busy with video guest appearances. During a rehearsal of her performance for Milton Berle's "Texaco Star Theatre" in 1952, Jeanette's perfectionism almost lost her the friendship of her TV co-workers. Constance Hope remembers the incident this way:

> She knew her business. She wanted it a certain way, she wanted the lighting to be just so, and they were kind of brushing her off, you know, "what do you know about lighting?"
>
> She stood her ground, and said, no, she wouldn't go on the program unless they lit her a certain way. She fought for it. Berle himself, and the producer and cast, were irritated at a star putting on airs. . . . But it was her business too, she had to look right.
>
> She held out for it. They lit her, and she looked absolutely beautiful. And they were so impressed themselves that they adopted her system. . . . She was almost always right when she insisted on something.

Also in 1952 the Raymonds began to spend more time in New York City. They rented an apartment on East 62nd Street. (Earlier they bid against Gertrude Lawrence for a triplex in the East Seventies.) Later Jeanette and Gene would transfer to 888 Park Avenue. They also acquired a villa on the Côte d'Azure, having become enchanted with the Riviera during their summer vacation there in 1951.

The Raymonds would make several Continental tours with their good friends, Constance (Hope) and Dr. Berliner. In Europe, Jeanette's popularity was still mighty. People would recognize her instantly on the streets, and she was always accommodating to her fans. Mrs. Berliner recalls Jeanette's generosity with everyone:

> One night [in Venice] we were taking them to a restaurant, a little fish place. . . . By the time we got there, there was already a stream of young people following us. They

164

recognized her. Then we went in, had dinner, it must have been about twelve. . . . We came out of the restaurant through the kitchen door, which is the way one went in, and there was a mob that filled the square, they had heard that she was there. She couldn't get in, she couldn't get out.

And so they began to say, "Cante, Cante, sing, sing." So she said, "I can't sing, no piano." "Cante, cante." By the kitchen door, she sang what they were screaming for, without a piano, without anything, and they went wild. I thought the whole place would fall in the water because they were so excited.

That same evening, the quartet went to another place for coffee and liqueur, where they were joined by other illustrious friends.

We happened to have Anton Dolan . . . and Markova, who were the two greatest dancers of that time. . . . Florence Walton was there. . . . She was the greatest ballroom dancer, and the team was . . . Maurice and Walton.

And when the music started, Pat [Dolan] got up and danced with Jeanette, and Gene danced with Alicia Markova, two of the great names in ballet, and we were all dancing out in the piazza . . . and the crowd was getting bigger and bigger.

In 1953 Jeanette became "Dr. Raymond" when Ithaca College presented her with an honorary Doctor of Music degree. She could now say she received her Ph.D. without attending college, based on what she learned in life! That same year she went to South America for a film festival. She was "so overwhelmed by fans" that she began to refresh her Spanish and was seriously thinking of undertaking a tour there.

Jeanette debuted in Las Vegas in the Fifties, appearing at various times at the Sahara Hotel and the Sands. She also performed at the Cocoanut Grove in Los Angeles, the nightspot where she and Gene had one of their earliest dates. Still a great drawing card, she continued to receive plaudits from the critics. Reported Margaret Harford in the *Hollywood Citizen News:* "Miss MacDonald's vitality and ageless

165

beauty are no small part of her glamour and she has plenty of glamour."

One of the most unpleasant experiences of Jeanette's life occurred in 1955, when she faced arrest in New York for being a negligent landlord. Magistrate Robert F. Mahoney signed a warrant for her on May 25, 1955, after she failed to appear after three postponements of a case involving fifteen violations of the housing law in a four-story building she owned at 52 West 97 Street in Manhattan. The building was considered a rooming house by the Department of Housing and Buildings. The authorities had decreed on March 17 that there were violations: "painted surfaces, dirty and unsanitary," "ceilings and walls plaster, dirty and broken."

Jeanette's attorney, Jerome M. Klein, stated in court, "She rented this West 97th Street building six years ago to a woman tenant, and the woman since has rented some of the rooms. Under the lease, this woman was to make any necessary repairs. In fact, I understand the minor violations complained of have been taken care of already."

Everything was eventually rectified, except for the bad memories it left Jeanette. Fortunately, that year had some pleasant times, as on September 4 through 6 when she appeared at the Sacramento, California, State Fair to participate in the Jerome Kern Tribute. She performed scenes, in costumes, from his repertory of operettas, including *Show Boat.*

The offers still came to Jeanette. Producers wanted her to star in a musical version of Gloria Swanson's movie hit, *Sunset Boulevard,* with the demented silent screen actress character changed to a song-stress. Jeanette declined the bid.

But on February 1, 1956, she did appear on "Screen Directors' Playhouse" in an episode entitled *The Prima Donna*. It was written especially for her by Gene and was a proposed pilot for a series. She told the press:

> Everybody tells me a series is hard work, but doing films for TV is almost the same as the motion-picture business, which I know well. And I'd like a chance at it. It's not like the terrible tension that exists in live television. Last time I did a live show I was a nervous wreck.

166

The series did not materialize, but later that year she agreed to be reunited with Nelson Eddy on a "Lux Video Theatre Special" entitled *Hollywood Musical History.* They sang one duet together which brought nostalgic tears to viewers. While many agreed that Nelson was still in fine voice, it was thought that Jeanette's tone was fading.

It was about this time that Jeanette's health started really to fail her. But she refused to relent. She joined with Gene in a "Playhouse 90" version of *Charley's Aunt* (CBS-TV, March 28, 1957) and later joined him on a trip to Europe. When she returned, she looked older and tired, with her thin body even thinner.

Yet retirement was not part of the MacDonald credo. She signed with a major New York publisher to prepare her autobiography. At one stage, she thought of titling it *Do Re Mi.* As she explained,

> I came to Hollywood frankly for the "dough"; when I was a star, I met the "Re"—Gene—and we were married; and then as Mrs. Raymond, I really found "me."

At another juncture she queried columnist friends:

> What do you think of my calling my autobiography *The Iron Butterfly?* It's one way of letting everybody know I know that's what some people call me. Besides, I think it'd sell copies.

She hired a writer to work with her, but it is reported that he became more interested in the cocktail hour than in the literary project. The book went through several drafts, but each time her publisher kept urging her to make it more spicy (which she would not do) and to abbreviate some of the earlier portions. The book became a way of life for her. At one point, before it was finally abandoned, she jokingly confided, "I have enough material for three volumes, but only one life to give my publisher."

Jeanette was fifty-five years old and ailing, but she refused to admit it. She appeared on such TV shows as "Queen for a Day" and Art Linkletter's "House Party," the latter to benefit the Cerebral Palsy Fund.

In the mid-Fifties she rediscovered another lucrative medium, the straw-hat circuit. She toured in *Bitter Sweet* and *The King and I* in the midwest. Her well-meaning operatic friends warned her that the strain of having to speak and sing a demanding role on a repeated schedule weekly would be very taxing. Could she handle it?

Yes. In fact, she found the experiences exhilarating. Often as she trekked from one theater to another, she would arrive at the new stage just in time for a 7:30 P.M. run-through and then, after a short midnight break, go through the full show again. She was always the perfectionist. The only problem she found in playing schoolmarm Anna was the costumes. As she confided to friend Clara Rhoades, long-time head of the Jeanette MacDonald International Fan Club, "By far the most strenuous part of the show was the sheer physical task of wearing Anna's costumes. Each weighed some thirty-five to forty pounds! I had to swirl around in them as if they were weightless fluff!"

If anything reminded Jeanette of the mortality of the human being, it was the passing of Louis B. Mayer on October 29, 1957, dead at age seventy-two of leukemia (others insisted it was of a broken heart at losing control of M-G-M). While many other contract stars at Metro would later defame the producer-chief executive, Jeanette always respected him as a businessman. She considered it an honor to sing "Ah, Sweet Mystery of Life" at his funeral.

In the summer of 1958 Jeanette sandwiched in a tour of Latin American countries, fulfilling an earlier ambition. The next July found her and Gene traveling to Sweden, where she discovered that the Scandinavians were as fond of her as of Jenny Lind.

Over the years Jeanette had not ignored her recording career. But it was only in the late part of 1957 that RCA Victor managed to convince her and Nelson Eddy to record a new series of selections to be entitled *Jeanette MacDonald and Nelson Eddy Favorites in Hi-Fi.* The numbers were mastered in New York and Hollywood in 1957 and 1958, with the orchestra under the alternate direction of Lehman Engel and David Rose. Among their duets on the LP were: "Will You Remember (Sweetheart)," "Indian Love Call," "Ah, Sweet Mystery of Life" and "Wanting You." She soloed "Giannina Mia," "Italian Street Song," "The Breeze and I," and "Beyond the Blue Horizon," while Nelson offered alone "Rosalie," "Rose-Marie," "While My Lady Sleeps," and "Stouthearted Men." The album was issued in 1959 and would eventually become a gold record album, making Jeanette and Nelson two of five people to win gold records for classical music. Actually "Indian Love Call" in 1959, after twenty-three years on the market, reached one million sales and earned a gold record distinction itself.

During the later Fifties Gene had kept professionally occupied hosting TV's "Fireside Theatre," returning to M-G-M for a featured role in the Jane Powell-Debbie Reynolds musical *Hit the Deck* (1955), playing Mercutio to Margaret O'Brien's Juliet and John Drew Barrymore's Romeo in Albert McCleery's production of the Shakespearean tragedy, and then going to Broadway—briefly—for *A Shadow of My Enemy,* with Ed Begley.

Then on January 30, 1959, the public learned how vulnerable Jeanette MacDonald could be. She entered Georgetown Hospital in Washington, D.C.

CHAPTER TWELVE

Jeanette was in the nation's capital to see Gene perform in a play when she was stricken and rushed to Georgetown Hospital. The physician in charge removed her appendix. She always insisted this was the beginning of her real physical problems.

She claimed that the operation had been unnecessary, that it was merely a matter of her having overeaten and experiencing stomach discomfort. After the surgery she was aghast when the doctor informed her, "While doing the operation I had your liver in the palm of my hand." As she would tell confidante Clara Rhoades, "How dare he have my liver out in his hand? What on earth do you suppose he was doing?"

A short time later she contracted hepatitis. But by Thanksgiving, 1960, she had sufficiently recovered to enjoy an "intimate" dinner with Blossom, Grace Newell and Gene in California. They had a few additions to the dinner table. Jeanette's minister (she was now an adherent of the Science of the Mind philosophy in Los Angeles) suggested that volunteers have foreign exchange students into their homes to celebrate the holiday. U.C.L.A. sent the Raymonds a French doctor, his wife and two young boys. Jeanette had to serve as both hostess and interpreter, as they spoke very little English.

People have got so fed up with sick pictures! Why don't they make one that says "God is love" instead of "God is hate"? And if they want to show a propaganda picture against war, why don't they remake *Smilin Through?*

The above were Jeanette's feelings on movies, 1960-style. As for modern music, she believed;

I find nothing sustaining or beautiful in much of the so-called popular music of today. You can't tell the melody, you can't tell the singer. Everything has a gimmick—everybody tries to be different. It takes more courage now not to be different.

Jeanette spent her birthday in June, 1961, very quietly. She had a small dinner party with Grace Newell (then eighty-six; she would die in 1966), two old friends and Emily. (Blossom, widowed for a year, was away for the weekend.) But a few days earlier, Jeanette celebrated in a bigger way. She and Gene gave a June-Bug party, asking as guests friends whose birthday was that month. Among the invitees were Charles Coburn, Gail Patrick Jackson, Richard Crooks, Elinor Warren, David Rose and Nelson Eddy. Gene composed special limericks to be inscribed on each of the special little birthday cakes. At the stroke of midnight, they drank a toast to Jeanette and Gene's twenty-fourth wedding anniversary.

In 1963 it seemed Jeanette and Gene might each be making films again. He was signed for a role in the Gore Vidal political drama *The Best Man,* released in 1964, and producer Ross Hunter sought Jeanette and Nelson Eddy for roles in his Doris Day comedy, *The Thrill of It All.* The singing operetta couple declined and the parts eventually went to Arlene Francis and her off-camera husband, Martin Gabel. Eddy proved to be the spokesman for the duo's refusal of that and other recent cinema offers. "We've been asked to do what might be called B pictures. Rather than do that, we decided to leave it on a high note."

Also in 1963, the Raymonds sold Twin Gables, deciding it was too difficult to continue finding proper help to maintain the house. They bought an apartment in western Los Angeles. Despite the flurry Jeanette made about decorating her new dwelling, Lloyd Nolan recently recalled for me, "Sadly enough, I don't think she was very happy there." Before the move from their home on a hill, they had to give away or discard a good many mementos they had accumulated over the years. It was a discouraging time for Jeanette.

When word of her continuing poor health filtered through to fan club members, Jeanette received a rash of get-well notes. But Jeanette was not one for sympathy. On September 11, 1963, she wrote Clara Rhoades:

> I have had quite a few personal letters from some of the members saying they are sorry I have not been feeling well and I feel that these thoughts are not healthy. Instead if they send thoughts to me and for me, as you do—of good health and energy, etc.—it has a more affirmative reaction. I am a firm believer in the power of prayer and good wishes and happiness and good thoughts, as against commiseration, and pity and all of the negative ideas that are floating around us. I am certain that is part of what is wrong with the world today.

In November of 1963, Jeanette, still ailing, was flown to the Methodist Hospital in Houston, Texas, where the noted heart surgeon, Dr. Michael DeBakey, performed an arterial transplant. The operation involved replacing an area of the aorta, the main artery leading from the heart, with a four-inch tube. After the operation, Jeanette developed pleurisy and had to remain at Houston Methodist for two-and-one-half months. The press was kept in the dark about her illness until the end of the hospital stay. In January of 1964, Jeanette returned to her newly-acquired condominium on Wilshire Boulevard, and continued her recuperation. Gene, meanwhile, had returned earlier to Hollywood to join Maurice Chevalier, Sandra Dee, and Andy Williams in a Universal movie entitled *I'd Rather Be Rich* (1964).

To cheer Jeanette up, friends would often invite her to join them at the Hollywood Bowl for concerts. They thought the music would uplift her spirits. On the contrary it would make her sad and wistful, especially when she would find the Bowl "barely filled." Of the Bowl,

1960s-style, she would remark sadly, "They don't understand. . . . I used to fill this place." In her heart, Jeanette knew that physically she could no longer do what she loved to do best.

Most of the Raymonds' friends did not realize the gravity of Jeanette's ailment. In December of 1964, shortly before Christmas, Jeanette was taken to the U.C.L.A. Medical Center, where she underwent abdominal surgery for adhesions. Jeanette remained in a hospital room there, with Gene by her side, until the end of the month. They were able to be home in time for a New Year's celebration.

But on January 11, 1965, Jeanette's health took a turn for the worse, as she was flown to Houston, Texas, on a commercial airliner, and taken to Methodist Hospital via ambulance for open-heart surgery. Dr. Michael DeBakey determined she was in "very critical condition" and decided to operate immediately. But this could not be done, as Miss MacDonald had grown too weak. She had to be fed intravenously. Gene was with her constantly.

During the next three days, Jeanette's condition seemed to improve a bit. Gene tried to instill encouragement in his wife. On Thursday, January 14, at about 4 P.M. she complained that her feet were cold. Solicitous, Gene began to massage them. Jeanette smiled in grateful appreciation.

A few minutes later she looked over at Gene and whispered, "I love you."

In a voice not much stronger than hers, he replied, "I love you, too."

With this, sixty-one-year-old Jeanette closed her eyes and died. It was 4:32 P.M. Central Standard Time.

CHAPTER THIRTEEN

On Friday, January 15, 1965, Jeanette's body was flown back to Hollywood. Among those grief-stricken was Nelson Eddy. Only a week earlier, he and Jeanette had talked on the phone and had made casual plans to get together soon. He had no conception of how gravely ill she had been. He told the press, "Many of the friends we worked with at M-G-M are gone. You accept it. But Jeanette MacDonald, you just can't accept it. . . . I'll never get over it."

On Monday, January 18, services were conducted for Jeanette at the Church of the Recessional at Forest Lawn Memorial Park. Dr. Gene Emmett Clark of the Church of Religious Science performed the services, and Lloyd Nolan read the eulogy.

The church was overflowing with 250 to 300 invited guests. Estimates are that from 2,500 to 6,000 people were milling about outside, while the services at the Glendale cemetery were underway.

A dazed Gene Raymond met the mourners before they entered the church, extending a hand to those as miserable as he.

Loudspeakers filled the air at Forest Lawn with several of Jeanette's most famous recordings, including "Ah, Sweet Mystery of Life." Seats were placed outside for Jeanette's fan club, as many members had journeyed from all parts of the globe to attend.

The active casket bearers, Senator Barry Goldwater (who had served with Gene during World War II), Robert Armbruster, Meredith Willson, General Lauris Norstad, Robert Ballin, Z. Wayne Griffin, Leon Ames and Nolan, were mournful servants of the ceremony. They filed past a long line of honorary casket bearers including Senator George Murphy, Colonel V. Bates, Joe E. Brown, Tom Cassidy, Sydney Guilaroff, Jose Iturbi, Otto Kruger, Robert Marlow, Michael McLaughlin, Colonel Frank Nye, Brigadier General J. E. Battley, Lew Ayres, Maurice Chevalier, Robert Fellows, Alfred Hitchcock, Cornwall Jackson, Ben Lyon, Lauritz Melchior, General Archie Olds, Colonel Donald Stout, Colonel Walter King, Giuseppe Bamboscheck, Nelson Eddy, Harold Grieve, George Garrett, Allan Jones, Nick Mayo and Dr. John Vincent. (Honorary pall bearers Dwight D. Eisenhower, Richard M. Nixon, Harry S. Truman, Chief Justice Earl Warren and Associate Justice Tom Clark could not attend and sent their regrets.)

Earlier that morning, sections of the park had been roped off by attendants, and mourners not directly invited to the services gathered in droves around the church.

The women were not all dressed in black; many had donned flowered dresses. Men wore typical California sportswear. Most of the fans were middle-aged, but more than one stroller was spotted in the crowd. According to those who make statistics of such events, Hollywood had not seen such a funeral since the death of Will Rogers three decades earlier.

Many friends and celebrities other than the above-mentioned persons attended the solemn occasion. A large number of the people who had witnessed Jeanette's marriage to Gene Raymond twenty-seven and one half years earlier were also present at the funeral. Among those who slowly filled the church pews were Mary Pickford and husband Buddy Rogers, Irene Dunne, Buddy Ebsen, Ralph Edwards, Greer Garson, Jane Powell, Cecilia Parker, Jack Oakie and of course, Blossom and Elsie.

Jeanette was laid to rest in a silk brocade gown. She lay in a metallic bronze casket, half open, covered with a blanket of pink roses. Inside the lid at the head was a bouquet of red roses. In her hands was the pink satin prayer book used at her marriage.

There were more than 140 floral tributes to Jeanette, so many that they overflowed the church's interior onto a side porch. Included among the flower pieces was a huge cross of white chrysanthemums and roses from Dwight and Mamie Eisenhower.

After an instrumental recording of "Beyond the Blue Horizon," Dr. Clark began the services. It was shortly after two P.M.

176

My friends, I want not so much to speak *to* you as to try to speak *for* you. It would be presumptuous for me to do otherwise. . . .

The truth within us all invites us not to bid farewell to our beloved Jeanette MacDonald, but to bid her Godspeed in her new experience in *life.* Jeanette MacDonald is not just that which lies here. Jeanette MacDonald is that which expressed *through* this body. . . .

No, Jeanette MacDonald is not this body. Jeanette is one of the loveliest forms of expression that God's life has ever taken. That life lived *in* this body. Jeanette is one of the ways God expressed the beauty of His Spirit. . . .

Think about the things you loved about Jeanette. They're spiritual things, really. Her warmth and graciousness. Her joy expressing as happy laughter—and then as music, as spontaneously as a bird would break into song. . . .

Jeanette MacDonald never played on stage or screen any love story so great as the *true* love story of her own life with her beloved and devoted Gene Raymond, her husband for twenty-seven years. But she had love enough to embrace us all—her friends, her audiences, the world who adored her. Perhaps she gave her heart to us more than we realized. . . .

Thank you, Jeanette, for putting something beautiful into our lives that we shall always cherish. God bless you. *We* love you, too.

After the playing of a recording of Jeanette's "Ave Maria," Lloyd Nolan, a good friend and a member of her church, delivered the eulogy.

We know how her name was emblazoned on screens and marquees throughout the world. We know that her glorious voice brought joy and delight to whole generations of people. Kings, princes, presidents—all sat entranced by the beauty of her song. . . .

Now, we must ask, why? There were other voices— other lovely faces. What was different about Jeanette? Why is hers the voice and the face we shall always remember? It was that last of her God-given gifts. It was her infinite capacity for love. Love for her devoted husband—love for her family and her friends. But even more, it was her love for the entire world that brought rapture to Jeanette's voice—and rapture to those who sat entranced and silent as her message of love poured forth. . . .

Now, she has gone to her heavenly Father, and her voice will join others in an angelic choir. But she will be with us still. As long as there are soft winds that caress the tops of tall trees—as long as there is sunlight on fields of swaying wheat—as long as there are moonbeams shimmering on blue-green seas—Jeanette will be with us, living in our memories and our hearts.

After a recorded version of Jeanette singing "Ah, Sweet Mystery of Life," Dr. Clark concluded the service.

May we now bless Jeanette in prayer, each according to his own faith and conviction, for it is written, "Have we not all one Father? Hath not one God created us?"

Jeanette was buried at Forest Lawn in the "Sanctuary Heritage" crypts. If one wishes to visit her final place of rest, one enters the building, turns right, and walks onward for approximately two passages. Jeanette is buried two sections from the top, near Nat "King" Cole and next to Alan Ladd.

It took most of the cars some eighty-five minutes to drive away from Forest Lawn.

EPILOGUE

Following her death, newspapers around the world published glowing tributes to the late singing star.

Allen York wrote in the *Chicago Daily Tribune:*

> The passing of Jeanette MacDonald makes us realize that the era of gay, lighthearted and romantic operettas on the silver screen is ended. Nelson Eddy and Jeanette MacDonald—there was a team! Her fragile beauty, dainty manner and magnificent voice were a heritage never to be forgotten, a heritage that abounds with the best melodic traditions of the movies.

The *Cleveland Press* lamented:

> Each generation has its own heroes and heroines, gods and goddesses who are wholly unknown to succeeding generations. Tell your children that Jeanette MacDonald died, and they will reply, "Who?"
>
> But those folks who have survived the Thirties will grieve and remember. They will remember her chirping merrily through *Naughty Marietta.* . . . They will remember that wherever Jeanette MacDonald sang, the stainless steel baritone of Nelson Eddy was sure to be there, too. Then, suddenly in 1937, the screen duet was over. Miss MacDonald

179

became Mrs. Gene Raymond, and in the most un-Hollywood manner, lived happily ever after as such—until her untimely death. . . .

In Hong Kong, a *China Mail* journalist answered the question "Why did Hollywood adore Jeanette MacDonald so much?"

I can quote a film scribe who has been covering the Hollywood beat since 1915. He said to me, "Jeanette MacDonald was one of the few people here who never said an unkind word about anyone. She was the same when she was right up there, and she is the same today. All she did brought credit to this city, and there isn't a nicer person here." It is nice to meet such success as Miss MacDonald enjoyed, and still be yourself. I remember her in the San Francisco earthquake scene singing the beautiful hymn "Nearer My God to Thee." Never, but never, have I known a cinema audience to be so stirred.

Perhaps the *Chicago Daily News* summed it all up best.

The older folks will mourn and remember Miss MacDonald and the young will never know what they missed.

The bulk of Jeanette's sizable estate was left to Gene. Nelson Eddy received a print of *Rose-Marie,* and Allan Jones a copy of *The Firefly* and the aforementioned silver dish. Mrs. Reni Willson (wife of Meredith) received a prized fan once owned by a Czarina. Jeanette's movie costumes, wigs, evening gowns, etc., were donated to the Music Academy of the West in Santa Barbara "in honor of my friend Lotte Lehmann." An antique harpsichord went to friend Robert Armbruster. Friend and secretary Emily West was to receive $400 monthly for life. Constance (Hope) Berliner was bequeathed an expensive set of china. Sister Blossom was to receive all of Jeanette's jewelry, while sister Elsie was left other personal mementos.

The legacy of Jeanette MacDonald's professionalism lives on in the movies and recordings (new compilations of her old 78 r.p.m. records are constantly being reissued), while her personal philosophy of a giving love has been carried on in the memory of Gene Raymond and through the deeds of the Jeanette MacDonald International Fan Club.

Jeanette MacDonald died on January 14, 1965. Many friends and co-workers followed her to the grave in the next few years. Nelson Eddy, while performing onstage in Florida, died of a stroke on March 6, 1967. On October 2, 1970, Jeanette's sister Elsie passed away. Death took composer Rudolf Friml on November 12, 1972. Sister Blossom, who has suffered several strokes, is now a patient at the Motion Picture County Home.

Gene Raymond, who has still not stopped grieving for Jeanette (he was unable to help with this biography for fear of "opening the floodgates of tears"), married Mrs. Bentley Hees on September 8, 1974, and now lives in Pacific Pallisades.

Each year devout members of the still-growing Jeanette Mac-Donald International Fan Club journey to California to pay tribute to Jeanette, and to hold a memorial service.

Of those who knew Jeanette well, the star herself was one of the last to realize her impact on the world and fame's special duties and rewards.

I never realized how much movie stars mean to people. Not what you do or what you say, but just your presence, your being there. It makes you feel embarrassed and rather humble and happy all at once. To be able to bring that much pleasure to people makes me a very lucky woman. Very lucky.